God on the Job

Finding God Who Waits at Work

by
THOMAS SMITH

PAULIST PRESS
New York/Mahwah, N.J.

Library of Congress Cataloging-in-Publication Data

Smith, Thomas, 1940–
    God on the job : finding God who waits at work / by Thomas Smith.
        p.   cm.
    ISBN 0-8091-3536-1 (pbk.)
    1. Work–Religious aspects–Christianity. 2. Witness bearing (Christianity) 3. Christian life–Catholic authors. I. Title.
BT738.5S65   1994
248.8′8–dc20   94-38491
                                                                      CIP

Published by Paulist Press
997 Macarthur Boulevard
Mahwah, NJ 07430

Printed and bound in the
United States of America

Contents

*To our twins, Kevin and Karla, who as young adults
are seeking their way in life.
May the love of God, the care of family, and the
support of friends bring them
comfort as well as challenge
joy more than pain
and wisdom along with knowledge.*

Introduction

At this stage in my life, I have already experienced a statistic I heard twenty-five years ago. I was convinced it was an exaggeration, one of those overstated predictions designed to get our attention but not even intended to be accurate. It was the statistical equivalent to literary license. But I remembered it. "Someone" (I can't remember who said it or what the setting was) claimed that average people twenty-five to fifty years from then would hold seven different jobs during their work life. Incredible! At the time, I didn't know anyone who changed jobs that often—unless, of course, he or she was irresponsible, lazy, abnormally restless, or all of the above.

Twenty years later as I look back on my own work history, I identify nine distinct major jobs. I began as a parish priest, then became a priest-teacher in a high school. After seven years, I applied for and received my laicization papers from the pope and took a job as a parish director of religious education. After five years I was selected as a diocesan director of education. Four years later I resigned and wound up selling cars. Within a year I was back in formal church ministry as diocesan director of RENEW and communications. Four years after that, I got a job at American Airlines as a program coordinator. I then became a manager of technical training and, four years later, a manager in the operations department, which is my current job. I sometimes wonder what I'm going to be when I grow up, or what I will be four years from now!

It isn't that these nine jobs are unconnected. A number of them are promotional progressions, and education in general is a consistent thread through many of them. But there are some major differences as well: the transition from classroom teacher

1

to administrator/director included a whole new set of skills and responsibilities. The change from religious education to technical training was much greater than I had expected. The move from training to operations was like moving to a new planet. Selling cars was like moving to a new galaxy! And beyond these nine jobs were the many different summer jobs I had when I was a student: laborer on a highway construction job and in a zinc manufacturing plant, dishwasher in a hospital cafeteria, maintenance worker at a school, census taker in the inner city, and a few I have conveniently forgotten.

I don't know how typical this brief resume is when compared with those of other people. But it strikes me that for many people the prediction that we will have seven different jobs in our lifetime is not as farfetched as I thought it was twenty-five years ago. In fact, my work history verifies the prediction. And I began my adult years with the absolute conviction that most people, certainly myself, would finish their work life doing basically the same thing they started with as a young adult. So goes one youthful "absolute conviction."

One advantage to my multi-job career is that it gives me a variety of job experiences to think about when I try to make sense of work. And in its most general terms, that's what this book is all about: making sense out of work. From this perspective, *God on the Job* is a personal journey. But frankly, if it were only a personal story, I doubt if too many people would be very interested. While I believe there are some intriguing chapters in this story—priest, teacher, salesman, manager—I don't think my individual tale is so engrossing that it's the stuff of a best seller, a mini-series or a network docudrama. I will therefore expand my theme and include comments from and about other people, and I will, at times, move from the personal experiential level and reflect on the meaning of this experience in the light of some basic Christian beliefs and values.

On the other hand, I will use personal examples and attempt to keep my theories tied to practical, everyday work situations that workers can easily identify. I challenge each reader/worker to take these written words and test them against his/her work experience. My hope is that these pages contain some ideas, reflections and experiences that will help workers, who are also believers, reconcile work and faith more completely. The extent to which this book reaches that goal is the extent to which this book is successful.

I know that this connection between work and faith is not an easy one. It hasn't been easy for me, even though for many years I worked in formal church ministry. For the past five years I have been attempting to join work and faith more closely in my own life, and I have discovered that I have never been very good at it, even in my formal church years. *God on the Job* reflects this work-faith journey and I am now much more comfortable with the relationship between work and faith in my own life. I certainly don't have it all worked out, and I probably never will! But I am much further along than I was a few years ago, and I hope you too make progress on discovering the God who is at work on your job. If you already experience *God on the job* in a truly meaningful way, then by all means write a book, hold a press conference, conduct a workshop or at least give me a call, because, I assure you, there are many believers who have difficulty integrating work and faith in any convincing way. And many of those believers *want* to put faith and work together more effectively. They simply don't know how. What is needed is a major dialogue on this topic. Some books have been written, some sessions held, some experiences shared, some efforts made, some insights discovered, some faith deepened. But much more is needed.

God on the Job is intended to contribute to this vital and emerging dialogue.

1

Work Is Work and Faith Is Faith

John Pearson is a friend of mine. I met him at the office when we worked on a few projects together. He's in a different department but we still see each other in the hall periodically, and we have lunch together occasionally.

The last time we had lunch the conversation somehow turned to religion and faith in general. We talked about our churches, our pastors and some personal faith experiences. The topic then turned to the company, our bosses and the economy. It was somewhat disjointed, like many lunch conversations are, but it was enjoyable. I also knew something was missing.

Driving home that evening it dawned on me that I was confused about a basic component of work and faith. I simply couldn't put the two together in any convincing way. The fact is I never really could reconcile work and faith. They seemed to be two different worlds, operating with two different sets of rules and basic assumptions.

Even when I was in formal church ministry, there was a separation between personal faith and planning and executing work activities. Many of those activities related directly to faith, God, church, sacraments and morality. These were the topics for a class, a workshop, a sermon or a meeting. It wasn't that my personal faith was so divorced from my ministry that everything I did was hypocritical. No. In fact, I was very sincere and genuine in the teaching or preaching I did. It's just that, on reflection many years later, I realize that teaching religion, preaching homilies, conducting parish meetings, and administering religious education programs is work very similar to the work I now do in a secular setting.

At the parish, meetings began with a prayer, and that was valuable. But once the meeting began, or the class started, or a program needed organizing, the actual work was very much like a meeting today to schedule the workload or initiate a new program or solve a myriad of work related problems. In other words, when I was a church minister, the topics were overtly religious, but the work process and the specific work activities were "secular."

This distinction is easier for me now that I work in a "secular" job. Without getting tangled up in the distinction between secular and sacred (and whether there is a clear distinction), it is simply clear to me now that work within formal church ministry is not all that different from work within secular settings. A church secretary is not unlike a company secretary. A church administrator is like thousands of other administrators. A pastor is a lot like a manager. A religion teacher is very similar to an English teacher. I admit that there are some differences in formal church work, but I am now much more impressed with the similarities in these job functions.

In other words, I believe that many people, including church ministers, are like me. We have difficulty integrating our work experience with our faith. Work is not viewed as contributing to faith. At best, we bring faith *to work*, and in this way live faith as much as possible in the workplace. But we either don't try or have become frustrated with understanding and accepting our work experience as potential for nurturing our faith and as a place for finding God.

God at Work?

"Go to work in order to find God?" you say. "You have to be kidding. Work is about the last place I would go to find God."

No, I am not kidding! And I don't think I am crazy. But

there are undoubtedly many people, including many believers, who share your skepticism. And I don't blame you! There are many valid reasons why we have trouble thinking of the workplace as a place to find God.

For example, when we leave work, we have many clear opportunities to foster and express our faith. The gates of the factory or the doors to the office are prison walls that refuse entry to the expression of faith. Outside those walls we are free to pursue faith expression in whatever area we choose. Even the trip home from work, whether by car, subway or bus, can become a time for explicit prayer, without interruption from work duties and responsibilities. Personally the drive to and from work is one of the best prayer times of the day for me. I call it "The Chapel of the Car." It's usually the most private time I have. Often, it's my best God-time.

When we get home, we can participate in formal church groups by joining a variety of church sponsored activities. Personal relationships with people who share similar beliefs can develop, and these informal relationships can be a source of both personal and religious support.

If we choose, we can attend Bible or religious study groups in order to deepen our understanding of our faith. We can become members of groups that share faith experiences. Or we can decide not to join any group and express our faith privately through prayer and personal study.

We can join other groups that nurture our spiritual lives. In my own case, my wife works as an alcohol and drug counselor. Our spiritual lives have been enriched by the twelve steps of Alcoholics Anonymous, a marvelous program that has opened the door to God, faith, and spiritual growth to millions of people. Many of us can find comfort and challenge in these kinds of groups.

Families can elect to participate in family religious education activities. Daily prayer, Advent and Lent home rituals, conversations about God, and explicit discussions on moral issues are common in these families. When children attend religious schools or religious education programs at their church, they often bring faith questions home, or their mere attendance leads to discussions related to faith and religion.

For example, our seventeen year old twins (a boy and a girl) have made a number of retreats this year and have obviously benefited from the experience. At home, it gives us a chance to talk explicitly about God and prayer.

We can also decide to become involved in faith-motivated social or political activities. We can devote a great deal of time and energy to those faith issues we believe are critical to public policy—issues like prayer in school, environmental concerns, civil rights, abortion, and peace.

Obviously, we don't have to choose all of these involvements. At one point in life we might be more inclined to one of these faith commitments. At another time, we might go in a different direction. Then again, we might decide to be uninvolved for a few years. Anyway, that's been my pattern. In any case, the point here is that we have the choice. In effect, in all areas of life except work, we are free to behave explicitly as believers.

Support for Faith

Not only are we free to express our faith but we have church support for many of these activities. In fact, many of these faith activities have become formal "ministries." Family ministry covers every aspect of family life. Youth ministry is available for support of teenagers. Lay ministry in general promotes the role of the laity both in the formal church and in the world. Social ministry provides an organized avenue of responding to the many economic, racial and social problems in our society. Ministry to the sick, for example, involves training and support for those of us who attempt to comfort the sick. Worship ministers, lectors, teachers in religious schools and religious education programs, church councils, committees, boards and clubs of all kinds usually have some support, encouragement and even training from local, or regional, churches.

But there is no work ministry.

This lack of attention is not surprising. In our current society, work is necessarily secular. For the most part, explicit references to faith are inappropriate. At times, individual workers may talk together about God, church and faith. Some may even meet regularly at lunch or before or after work for prayer, study or discussion. Workers may pray privately while on the job. Where I work, one of the staff assistants reads the Bible during lunch time. But even in these presumably rare cases, work is work and faith is faith.

Those of us who try to apply faith principles to our work life generally run into difficulty and confusion. I know I do. The forces at play in the workplace are not easily identified as consistent with religious values. The necessary emphasis in private industry on profit and productivity, particularly in a recessionary economy but also present when economic times are good, tends to obliterate all other forces that could be readily interpreted as expressions of the presence of God. The large segment of our society that works for the federal, state or local governments is constantly concerned about funding, election results and the inevitable political ramifications of the department or agency. The presence of God and the exercise of faith get lost in the midst of these overriding forces.

Check it out with your own work experience. Isn't it true that integrating your faith with your work is not easy? Most of us don't really integrate faith and work. We accommodate; we adjust, and ultimately we accept the assumption that work and faith just don't fit together very well.

The deal goes something like this: we express and nurture our faith at home, within our congregations or in the privacy of our own thoughts and prayer. We go to work and try to be as consistent with our beliefs as we can. If we like our work and the people we work with, we feel fortunate and chalk it up to luck. If, like most people, we don't like our work or the people, we try to accept the situation with as much patience as possible. The boredom and hassles that inevitably emerge in every job are included in the "suffering in life" category. We may concentrate on keeping a positive attitude, believing that the best we can do in a difficult situation is to look on the brighter side and to offer up the suffering as part of the sacrifice demanded of all believers.

On the other hand, we may just hate our job. The resentment, anger, and dissatisfaction are a destructive part of our daily life. Perhaps the job itself is intolerably boring, the boss is a genuine jerk, company policies are overtly ridiculous, and co-workers are irredeemably insensitive. Or maybe the job is basically accept-able, but we simply don't like giving up eight hours a day, five days a week doing what we do. There are other things we would rather do during much of that time. So, we resent our work, at least occasionally.

Whatever the reason, many of us don't like our jobs. How we handle this resentment and bitterness varies from person to person. Most of us learn to live with it because we see no realistic alternative. Some of us get different jobs, which may or may not alleviate our dissatisfaction. Some of us fight by trying to make changes in the workplace that we believe will help our situation. Some of us seek a relatively acceptable compromise because we need the money. Some of us just accept the situation and seek enjoyment and "meaning" in other parts of our life.

In the midst of all these immediate emotions and concerns, we don't even consider the relationship between faith and work. That relationship is thought to be too far removed from the real issues about coping with work.

This separation of work and faith starts immediately upon employment. When we begin with a company or move to a new department we pick up the prevailing attitudes within the group. We are concerned about being accepted and learn-ing what is expected. Faith is never a part of the work culture and, as a result, it is taken for granted that faith is not a significant factor in performing job responsibilities and establishing work relationships. As a new employee, we inherit a culture that ignores faith.

There is, therefore, little opportunity to attempt a positive integration of work and faith. In other societies, this integration is taken for granted. In countries that sponsor a particular religion, explicit references to religious beliefs are not only permitted but they are demanded and non-compliance is punished. There are specific religious practices that are required during the day, holydays become holidays, and religious orthodoxy is a criterion for success on the job.

Many other countries, like the U.S.A., have determined that the dangers of a state imposed religion are too great a threat to individual liberty and have chosen to adopt a type of society that protects freedom of religion. This approach has created a better society in terms of protecting individual rights and maintaining a system of law that, on balance, has done quite well for the majority of citizens. Constitutional law that rejects the specific tenets of any particular religion has the best chance of being fair to all members of a pluralistic society.

As a consequence of this approach, those of us who are believers must restrict overt faith expression and practices to our non-work lives. The positive side of this position is that non-believers, or believers of a different affiliation, are protected from the imposition of beliefs. The downside of this experience is that we are left to our own devices to figure out how to integrate work with faith. If we attempt this process, we discover that this integration is not easy and most of us then look for assistance.

Where do we look?

Work and Faith: Church Support?

Usually we turn to our church for faith support. And generally the churches offer this support in some form or another for family issues, religious education, youth, social problems, etc. But what happens when the focus turns to work? Not much.

Some homilists occasionally urge the congregation to act like believers at work or to follow general moral directives when doing their job. There's a periodic reference to working conditions and the responsibility of employees to do a "full day's work for a full day's pay." The admonition is coupled with a similar reminder to employers to respect the rights and dignity of their workers.

That's about it. And even if there is an exceptional occasion when work and faith are the main theme of a homily, the assumption is that we believers need to "bring faith to the workplace" in order to manifest those beliefs as best as possible in a hostile environment.

This observation about preachers is not a condemnation. It is just that—an observation. The dichotomy between faith and work is long lasting and deeply entrenched, and homilists usually share the perspective that the factory, store or office is not fertile ground for finding the presence of God. I admit that when I was preaching regularly, I thought of the workplace as a very remote arena for God's activity. I concentrated on what I knew: scripture, sacraments, theology, church. My homilies reflected my knowledge and experience. They were pretty good homilies, too, if I must say so myself. (Which I probably do since I doubt if anyone remembers much of what I said!)

I don't think many of my priest friends approached the issue of work and faith much differently than I did. We learned in theology class that work and especially workers had dignity, but we didn't explore the relationship between work and faith very deeply.

I don't think things have changed too much in this regard. I seldom hear homilies that address real work related issues. When I do, the homilist is usually and significantly a permanent deacon who also has a "secular" job. But for the most part, the relationship between faith and work is still not a major theme emanating from the pulpits of the world.

Therefore, if we search for a richer reflection on work and faith, we become discouraged, and since most of our friends aren't even asking the question about faith and work, we give up and join the vast majority of people who assume that faith at work is really out of place anyway. Our society has dictated that life must be compartmentalized, with the largest isolated compartment reserved for work. It is extremely difficult to think otherwise.

Church Teachings on Work and Faith

We can turn to church teachings on the relationship between work and faith. Catholics, and many other believers who take the time, will find help in some papal encyclicals. Other denominations can surely find similar documents and teachings. Unfortunately, these teachings are not read sufficiently. "Ordinary lay people" figure these writings are hard to understand and downright boring. But these documents offer rewarding guidance. For example, beginning with Pope Leo XIII's "Rerum Novarum" in 1893 and including Pope John Paul II's reflections in more recent letters, we can find many passages which outline the rights of the worker, the deplorable nature of some working conditions, the demands of justice and the responsibilities of owners to treat employees fairly. There are sections that also describe the fundamental dignity of work and, even more often, the fundamental dignity of the worker. These teachings are consoling and enlightening to the serious believers who study these documents and seek to apply them in their lives.

But there are a few complications. First of all, these writings are primarily teachings, written to clarify the implications of the gospel as it applies to working conditions. As such, these letters are not written in a style that easily relates to our spiritual life. Secondly, these documents, of necessity, must address worldwide issues in broad terms. As a result, we are still left with the formidable task of integrating and incorporating these principles into our own work experience and

faith. It is precisely this process of integration and incorpora-
tion that we find difficult. And it is precisely that process
where there is little practical assistance.

The main difficulty, then, with formal church documents
like the papal encyclicals is not the letters themselves, nor
even their writing style. The primary problem is that the pop-
ularizers—the theologians, spiritual writers, educators and
preachers—have not struck a responsive note among ordinary
believers. The call for better working conditions and the
rights of workers has been heard in many circles, and there
has been some measurable improvement in these areas in
many parts of the world. But the underlying theme that work
itself has value in terms of building God's kingdom is largely
ignored, both theoretically and practically. Those populariz-
ers, and there are some, who do deal with this issue don't
have a very large audience, primarily because the dichotomy
between faith and work is so ingrained that most people are
not easily attracted to this theme.

To a large extent, therefore, we are left to our own devices.
That fact plus the prevailing and almost universal assumption
that work and faith are not supposed to unite in any integral
way makes it extremely difficult to integrate these two parts
of life.

That fact, of course, doesn't mean that the effort is useless,
or the rewards insignificant.

An Integrated Life

I am making an assumption here. I am assuming that I, and
other believers, want an integrated life and that faith is a critical element in that integration. It sounds right to say, "Yes, of
course, I want an integrated life. Who doesn't?" But, to be
honest, it's easy enough to live with a certain amount of disintegration. I have done it, and continue to do it. It's a matter of
degree. Total disintegration means psychosis; total integration
means heaven. We are all somewhere between these polls. An
integrated life implies a unity among the physical, emotional,

spiritual, social and intellectual aspects of life. That's a large order. I have moments, even days, when I feel like those five pillars of life are all connected. But then one or more of them gets out of line. I get angry at some incident at work and I let it eat at me, destroying my unity. I have a hassle with my wife or kids, and I nurture my hurt feelings and disappointment. I drift away from prayer, take God for granted and feel a vague emptiness that robs me of peace. I withdraw emotionally from the events and people around me until someone or something jolts me back to meeting life head-on again.

None of these experiences are so bad that my life falls apart, or I am unable to keep going with my personal and professional responsibilities. But my life varies: at times I feel together, and at other times I feel parts of me are slipping away, not properly connected. You, too?

I experience at least two levels of life. One is on the surface and one is deeper. The surface includes getting out of bed, working, checking with the family schedule, eating meals, doing chores, going to movies, most conversations, shopping, watching TV and almost everything else! The deeper level includes some prayer, worship and meditation (but not always!); some discussions about feelings (mine and other people's), life principles and goals, truth, beauty, good and evil, some political issues; doing some projects (like writing this book or completing some project at work that I really get into); some group experiences that mysteriously move beyond the surface.

Is your experience similar? Probably. Different events and interests attract different people and therefore the specifics will vary, but we all have a surface life and a deeper life. Furthermore, the five major pillars of life—physical, emotional, spiritual, social, and intellectual—all have a surface level and a deeper level. The possibilities then are myriad: I can be on the surface in all five areas simultaneously and live 90% of my life this way. I can be at a deeper level intellectually but remain on the surface on the other four levels. I can be deeper emotionally, spiritually and socially, and remain on the surface physically and intellectually. I will, of course, move in and out of these levels, sometimes very much on the surface and sometimes deeper. I may be comfortable at a deeper level in one category (e.g. social) and very uncomfortable in a different category (e.g. spiritual).

Integrated people are those who experience a unity among these five aspects of life at both the surface level and at the deeper level. They don't always live at the deeper level in all five areas simultaneously, but they experience a deeper level in all areas. They also reflect on these experiences. Therefore, there is a core unity among their many activities: family, recreation, work, church, neighborhood, civic community, school, etc. They relate comfortably and perform acceptably in all of these arenas. They experience consistency and unity. It is clear to them and to others that the one same person performs these various functions. That's an integrated person.

Some unifying principle, goal, experience or relationship is needed to pull this multi-faceted life together. The more integrated a person is, the more connected are the physical, emotional, spiritual, social and intellectual parts of life. Disintegration means that one or more of these pillars of life, at either the surface or a deeper level, is not basically consistent with the other parts of life. When the unifying element is missing or unclear, disintegration in some degree will appear.

For Christian believers, the centerpiece of this integration is faith in Jesus. How that faith is expressed will undoubtedly vary from Christian to Christian. Some people are Christian in name only, perhaps born into a Christian environment that is more cultural than genuine. The Mafia is an extreme example: they are committed to power, greed, murder, theft, and intimidation and yet all of this evil is surrounded by a veneer of Catholic ritual and language. To claim Christianity or to use religious language is not a guarantee of faith.

Regardless of where you and I are on the continuum between sinner and saint (and we're some of both!), we have chosen to put faith in Jesus at, or at least near, the center of our life. Our general interpretation of life, our basic under-standing of what makes life meaningful, includes an explicit reference to our faith in Jesus. Some of you may identify Jesus as the source of meaning for every specific life detail you experience. Some of you may rarely speak about Jesus directly. You may believe that faith is lived in deed more than in word and are uncomfortable using explicit religious language. The frequency of direct references to Jesus, the Bible or God is not the criterion for judging the intensity or authenticity of Christian faith. God cannot be fooled, and only God can judge the sincerity of faith. And while sincerity is critical to authen-tic faith, sincerity is not the criterion of truth. Believers can sincerely believe in something or someone that is simply not the truth. In any case, there are many acceptable styles of faith.

The Divided Life

Regardless of style, authentic faith is a source of integration. On the other hand, its easy enough for us believers to be con-tent with a compartmentalized life. In it's clearest form, this divided life implies that faith is left for Sunday morning, work is another life that goes from eight to five during the week, weekends and evenings are still another life. It's possible to lead these three separate lives, and many variations among them, without too much difficulty and without clinical schizo-phrenia. In fact, our culture supports this approach. Leave work at work. Leave family issues at home. Leave God in church. Leave school at school. Recreation and entertainment have another niche. To go from one to the other is not a major problem.

In our society, there are no predictable disastrous conse-quences to a divided life. We believers are not exempt; we too can successfully navigate these various rivers and lakes of life.

Integration, then, is not like a light switch which is either off or on. It is more like a dimmer switch which controls the brightness of the light.

The assumption here is that many of us want to turn up the dimmer switch a little brighter but we don't know how. The switch is too complicated, and the operating manual cannot be found. We may pray about it and have some ideas, but we don't have the confidence or direction to move to the next level of a life more integrated around our faith.

And, to repeat what I said earlier, work is often the most difficult part of life to incorporate into a truly unified life. Hopefully, the rest of this book will shed some light on how this integration of work and faith can take place.

Meaning-Makers and Meaning-Finders

Many people have rightly stated that human beings are meaning-makers. We *bring* meaning to life. Each of us has an individualized view of the world; no one sees the world exactly as I do or you do. Every event we experience, every feeling we have, every thought we think—each and every one of them is filtered through a unique vision. The meaning we attach to these events is ultimately very personal.

How these meanings are developed is a complex and extremely important process. The culture, media, friends, family, teachers, religious institutions—they all have influence on this process. In one sense, meaning is given to us. How to interpret an event, how to identify and state a feeling, how to think about an idea is handed to us by willing external sources. Sometimes these messages are clear and unanimous; sometimes they are confused and contradictory.

We receive these messages and, consciously or subconsciously, we accept, reject or modify their meanings. What emerges is a gathering of meanings. Some people are able to consciously arrange these meanings in a relatively reasonable order and are able to communicate this order with some degree of accuracy. These are the people who "know themselves." Other people receive these meanings and are barely aware of the influence or the message. Without reflecting on these constant "in-puts," or even admitting there is a need to reflect, some people adopt the meanings from external sources as their own.

In either case, some internal processing takes place. Aware, reflective people have greater control over what they adopt and how they arrange the messages in terms of importance and what appropriate actions should be taken and what feelings are consistent with the incoming meanings. Unaware and unreflective people accept these external meanings uncritically and attempt to deal with the inevitable conflicts and confusion as best they can. In fact, one definition of insanity is the inability to process these conflicting meanings successfully. However, both reflective and unreflective people experience some form of internal activity which, in general, is designed to process these continuing messages about life.

Because of this internal process, we are rightly called meaning-makers. Some people say that we are the exclusive creators of our own meaning. The only meaning we possess is self generated, either as "borrowed" and shaped from external sources or as created as an original interpretation of some aspect of reality. Each of us, therefore, brings meaning to life, i.e. there is no meaning in external events or people until a person "puts" meaning there.

There is no doubt that we create and bring meaning to life. There is no doubt that clarification of this meaning is vital to self-knowledge, and emotional maturity, and is a critical tool in dealing with life's many problems. There is no doubt that our personal faith is a powerful meaning-maker in that faith creates a transcendent, fundamental interpretation of life. There is no doubt that we can alter our interpretations of life, to change the meaning of events and experiences and to view life with new perspectives. There is no doubt that these new perspectives can be either positive or negative. There is no doubt that we create meaning in life, even when we are unable to articulate this meaning.

But we are more than meaning-makers. We are also meaning-finders. If I were only a meaning-maker, I would be locked within a subjective universe from which there is no escape. My world and my meaning would have no connection with an "outside world," if it even existed. I would have no confidence in sharing my meaning with others because, in the final analysis, all meanings would be so individualized they could not be shared.

Reality, then, includes an "outside world" that we can access. We can, in varying degrees, make contact with this outside world. We are meaning-makers, but the meaning we make is a reflection on something or someone who is really there. My personally created meaning is accurate insofar as it accurately reflects the reality that exists independent of me. In other words, some meaning pre-exists my experience of creating my internal meaning. I am also a meaning-finder.

This insistence on the reality and importance of a world independent of my interpretation of that world is critical when faith is considered. Christian faith demands the existence of a God independent of me. God is not just a projection of my interpretation of reality. God is, and God is somehow "present" in and to the world. From the Judeo-Christian perspective, God is within us, but God is also outside us. Christianity is an uncompromising "both/and" faith: God is *both* beyond me and within me; God is *both* transcendent and immanent, both almighty and approachable, creator *and* redeemer, just *and* merciful.

This "both/and" theme carries into the issue of meaning. I *bring* meaning to life but I also *find* meaning in life. For example, I enjoy basketball. I bring my meaning to the game because I played it for many years, enjoyed the competition and challenge, and I respect the individual and team skills needed to perform well. I bring meaning because I have been a fan for years, coached at the elementary school level for a number of years and talked about players and plays for most of my life. Yes, I definitely bring meaning to basketball.

But I also find meaning in the game. There is a logic, an order, a dynamic that exists completely independent of me.

The rules, history and popularity of basketball has its own meaning and life regardless of my participation or interest. I can focus exclusively on my subjective experience of basketball and my meaning is then totally personal. Or I can choose to discover, nurture and celebrate the objective side of the game and add this dimension to my current experience of basketball. If I choose to broaden my perspective, my appreciation of the game increases. When I both bring and find meaning in events and experiences, I experience life more fully.

One more example: I bring meaning to my relationship with our children. This meaning is generated by many complex factors, including conception, pregnancy, birth, infancy, childhood, adolescence. At this point over seventeen years of expectations, memorable events, shared moments, difficult times, fun times, pride, some anger, adjustments, delights... and much more. I have created some meaning out of all of this, some meaning that relates to me as a parent, as a spouse, as an individual. That's my personal meaning—that's what it means to me. I'm not able to analyze it all or spell it out or state it all clearly, but I know it's there. Undoubtedly, I bring meaning to my role as parent.

But I also find meaning in my children. They exist apart from me. Their personalities go beyond what I have brought to them. As close as we are, their world is separate from me. If I choose, I also discover meaning in them that is quite independent of me. There is something richer, deeper, more mysterious and rewarding if I seek their meaning as independent human beings as well as my own subjective perspective. It's not an either/or situation; it is a both/and experience. But to experience the both/and, I have to be willing and able to "let go" of my purely subjective approach to parenthood.

Applying this same principle to the relationship between work and faith implies that I both bring faith to work and find God at work. When we think of "God on the job," we assume we mean that we bring God to work. That's true, but we also can find God at work and through work. And it's this part of the experience that is the focus of this book. How can we find God at work? And if we do, what can we do about it?

Most basically, God is present everywhere and therefore God is also present at work. Regardless of my being at work or your being at work, God is already there. God is present in co-workers. God is also present in the activity, the culture, the environment that is work. God is present at work no less than God is present at home, in church activities, in society in general. Some actions offer an intense channel of Godpresence. But the intensity of the presence during these encounters does not deny nor diminish the real presence of God in other activities, including work.

Faith is necessary to find the pre-present God. We believers are more or less skilled at finding that presence at home, in church activities, in some personal experiences, in scripture, and even in social or political events. But we are not as skilled at finding Godpresence at work.

It is difficult to find God at work, if the assumption is that God isn't really there anyway. And for all practical purposes, that is precisely the assumption.

Work is the place where most of us spend about half of our waking hours. Very little theology or spirituality has focused on the work experience as such. There's probably many reasons for this unfortunate lack of attention. As a matter of fact, most theologians and spiritual writers generally don't work in the secular world. And while their reflections would be most helpful, it's also important to solicit workplace theologians to address the relationship between work and faith in theoretical and practical detail. Permanent deacons are one theologically trained group who are already bridging this gap between work and faith. They also have the advantage of access to pulpits where this theme can regularly get to us believers in the pews. Lay ministers of many varieties, many of whom have completed theological studies, can turn their attention to faith and work. Working together with the clergy on a regular, sustained basis, we can identify, nurture and celebrate Godpresence at work.

Until we are able to integrate work and faith by finding God, and meaning, in and at work, we will not have an integrated, mature faith. The integration is not just a matter of bringing faith to work; it is even more a matter of discovering the Godpresence that is already there. This is serious business because if I am able to harmonize all other areas of my life with faith except my work life, I am not a complete believer. We cannot be content with the prevailing separation between work and faith. Workfaith needs to move closer to the center of our life.

Study Questions

1. Opening Exercise:
   Each participant responds to the following questions:
   (Each person takes no more than a total of five minutes.)

   A. What does the company/agency you work for do? What is the company's mission?

   B. What is your role at work?

   C. What do you like about the job?

   D. What do you dislike about the Job?

2. In your opinion, why do you think there is little attention focused on the relationship between work and faith?

3. What is the difference between faith and morals/ethics when applied to work?

4. In terms of work and faith, what similarities do you see between people who are paid to work and people who are not formally employed, e.g., retired people, the sick, home-makers, the voluntarily unemployed, etc.? How can these formally unemployed people benefit from a clearer under-standing of the relationship between faith and work?

2

Workfaith

Is God at work? All work? Every job? All the time?
Yes!
End of chapter?
Perhaps it should be. Presuming to know how God works
is dangerous business. We mortals are somewhat like God and
a whole lot unlike God. What I say about God is therefore filtered and limited by my many inherent inadequacies.

On the other hand, I presume to say something about God
only because I believe, along with other Christians, Jews,
Muslims, Buddhists and various other religions, that God has
chosen to reveal some things about who God is, what God
wants and how God works.

I am a Christian, and therefore I believe that this God communication has its focus in Jesus Christ who is both divine
and human. This revelation continues in scripture, church
teaching, the authentic inspiration of the Holy Spirit, nature,
ritual actions, and even other people. Even though something
can go wrong in all of these avenues of divine communication, enough God-truth gets through to make some confident
statements about who God is, what God wants and how God
works. It's true that scripture can be misinterpreted, church
teaching can be misunderstood, inspiration of the Holy Spirit
can be confused with self messages, nature can be taken for
granted, ritual actions can be ignored, and other people—
well, other people can be unreliable. But we can still know

significant things about God because some of the truth about God makes it through the obstacles we set up and the limitations we possess.

In other words, while it's true that what we don't know about God is far more than what even the most ardent believer does know about God, it's also true that even the slightest knowledge about God can clarify the meaning of life.

So, insisting that I know something about how God is present in the workplace is dangerous business. I therefore proceed cautiously, but with enough confidence to, in fact, proceed.

Yes, God is present at work, every job, all the time.

This belief is an extension of the basic position that God is everywhere. It is the nature of God to exist, and since God is God, God exists everywhere. Anywhere something is, God is also there.

Actually, there's only three choices. We can believe that there is a God, or that there is not a God, or that we don't know if there is or isn't a God. If we believe there is a God, once again, there are only three possibilities: there is a loving God, a hostile God, or an indifferent God. Regardless of how we perceive God, the "real" God can only be loving, hostile or indifferent. Pulling away all the nuances (which may be very significant), those are the only true alternatives.

In case there is any doubt, I believe in the existence of a loving God. How this existence is understood and this love is manifest becomes more complicated, but the basic fact of this belief is my starting point. A loving God exists.

And this is the God who is everywhere. But what does God do every day? Does God just hang around, occasionally popping unannounced into someone's life or some major current event? In other words, if God is present everywhere, *how* is God present? More specifically, *how* is God present in and at work?

These questions can't be answered in one word. Presence,

any presence, and especially Godpresence, is real but elusive, evident but undefinable, and essential but assumed.

An analogy is helpful. Radio waves are in the air, everywhere. I can't explain how they got there, what they do from the perspective of physical science, or how they move from one point to another. But I know these radio waves exist. I also know that turning on and tuning in a radio will translate these waves into intelligible sound. Knowing how and why that translation takes place is not important to me. To listen to a specific program, all that is important is that the proper waves exist in the immediate air and that I have a radio capable of tapping into those waves.

Presence, including Godpresence, is something like radio waves. God is there, just as the waves are there. But God, of course, is also unlike the waves, particularly since God is creator and personal, while the waves are created and impersonal. The analogy does illustrate, however, the existence of something that is generally elusive, undefined, and assumed, which at the same time is real, evident and essential.

To look further into Godpresence, it is valuable to look at human relationships. We can project what we know about human presence onto God, not because God is just like humans, but because humans are created by God "in his image and likeness" (Gn 1:27). There are traces of godlikeness in humans, and features like intelligence, choice, and love are aspects of human life that more closely resemble features of God. Presence is another of those characteristics. Since God's nature is to exist, presence is incorporated into existence. Presence implies that God created something or someone to whom the existing God is present. For all practical purposes God's existence includes presence.

Degrees of Presence

I experience degrees of presence. There are times when I am aware of a "moment of intensity" in a relationship, when I feel more present to another person. Sometimes it's a friend:

we spend time together, with undivided attention and focused on feelings, questions, concerns or plans that are very personal and significant. Some of these times are moments of intensity in the relationship, occasions which deepen the friendship and foster greater trust, respect, care and understanding. There is an experience of greater presence to each other during these times than during times when we are together on a more surface level. When the topic is not as immediately personal, when the event we are sharing is externally stimulated (like a movie), when we are visiting other people, when we don't feel like putting more personal energy into a conversation—in all of these situations I feel present to my friend but not to the same degree of intensity as when we openly deal with our most personal thoughts and feelings.

It's the same way in my relationship with my wife. We have moments of intensity in our presence to each other. Other couples say the same thing. The wedding day, the birth of children, special family events, some conversations, some vacations, some sexual experiences, some quiet time—these are all events of personal, memorable, and intense presence.

My spiritual journey follows the same pattern. Some times at prayer, during the reception of the sacraments, when reading the Bible, when visiting other people, when visiting nature, some times very privately and some times very publicly—I know that I have had moments of spiritual intensity when I was sure that God was calling me, comforting me or present to me in a way that went beyond my normal experience of Godpresence. And I know I am not alone in this experience.

In terms of presence, we simply do not experience life evenly. There are peaks and valleys. There are moments of intensity.

There are even times when I feel present to someone who is absent. A card, a phone call, a photograph, a long cherished letter, a thought can activate feelings and thoughts of another person to such an extent that the person "feels" present. By the same token, people who are physically present can be ignored to such an extent they "feel" absent. Physical presence is not a guarantee of intense presence, and absence is not an indication of lack of presence.

Degrees of Godpresence

Since these degrees of presence are so basic and pervasive in human experience, it is legitimate to assume that Godpresence also admits of degrees.

What's more, these degrees of Godpresence are intended on God's part and not just due to the limitations imposed by human nature. The divine nature as it relates to itself is, by definition, never changing. To be God means to be intensely and completely God at all times in ways that are unimaginable to us. But God can, and seemingly has, chosen to communicate with people in degrees. Miracles, for example, are moments of intense Godpresence that are beyond the normal Godpresence.

There are also events that Christians recognize as moments of intensity on God's part. In God's love affair with us, these special encounters are high points in the relationship between God and us. They are moments of intensity precisely because other moments are not as intense. The uniqueness of these encounters does not undermine the belief that all of the universe is fundamentally sacramental, that is, that Godpresence is always and everywhere somehow reflected in this material world. These special occasions are opportunities for believers to meet God who is present in a unique way. Baptism, for example, is one of these moments of intensity. While different Christian denominations disagree about certain aspects of baptism, we all agree that this ritual action is a moment of extraordinary contact between God and us.

Occasionally we testify to peak, personal religious experiences that go beyond our normal experience of Godpresence. One interpretation of these experiences is that we are more "open" to receiving Godpresence at these times. That may be true, but it doesn't seem to explain everything. The other part of the explanation at least implies that God is more "active" during these peak experiences. What does a "more active God" mean? Isn't God always completely active?

When relating to people, it seems not. God chooses to be more "active" at some times with certain people than at other times with other people, or even with the same people.

The conclusion becomes obvious: even on God's side, there are moments of intensity in Godpresence. What's more, we don't seem to have much control over these moments of intensity. Miracles are primarily God's work, and even though an element of faith is present, sometimes it appears that God acts in a special way simply because God chooses to do so. Faith healers tend to stress their own personal power to get God to heal. But God is not the healer's servant, doing what the healer wants. God does what God wants, when and how God chooses. God may hear the prayers of faith healers and anyone else, but the kind of action that results from that prayer is not initiated by the pray-er but by God. God acts; we respond. We request; God decides.

Similar comments can be made about encounters with God and peak religious experiences. We generally must do our part to prepare for and accept the intense presence of God. Personal faith, the focus of attention, the elimination of distractions, are usually necessary to properly receive the more intense moments of Godpresence. But it remains true that the experience of intense Godpresence is not always attributable to our readiness. God relates to us in varying degrees and God remains in charge of these experiences.

On the other hand, certain conditions are conducive to intense Godpresence. If we never participate in sacraments with an active faith, most likely we will not experience Godpresence intensely in the sacraments. If we don't accept the possibility of miracles, we will probably not accept a specific miracle even when it's close to us. If we explain peak experiences in emotional or psychological terms only, presumably we will not claim a "religious" experience.

There are exceptions: Paul's conversion on the road to Damascus, Abraham's original call, Jesus' forgiveness of the good thief, etc. These events are exceptions, and they illustrate that God is in charge and makes decisions that we can't predict or control. Despite these exceptions, certain circumstances are more conducive to intense Godpresence than others.

Families who pray and express their faith openly and honestly generally have a greater opportunity to respond to Godpresence than a family who denies God, neglects prayer and fosters negative feelings toward each other. If you know yourself, your strengths and weaknesses, and if you accept your limitations with honesty and sincerely want to become more loving and a better believer, then you are more likely to respond to Godpresence than people who remain self-centered and harbor negative feelings toward themselves and others. If you associate with other believers who are genuinely striving for greater faith and better love, you will probably hear God's word more clearly than people who associate with others who ignore God and foster hatred, prejudice, materialism and selfishness.

Obviously, the presence of God is more complex than a simple yes or no. On both God's part and our part, presence is experienced in degrees.

Godpresence at Work

What degree of Godpresence do we find at work?

God is more actively and intensely present at work and in work than what most of us assume.

It's easy enough to make that statement because most of us assume that God isn't present at work anyway. Or, if we agree that God is everywhere, even at work, that generic presence doesn't amount to much. What is God's job description and how come we don't consider God on the job?

For many of us, life is so compartmentalized that our faith

is also compartmentalized. A personalized, active faith at home, at church and in social activities can become deactivated and impersonalized in the workplace. As a result, we can become inadvertent Deists on the job. Deists believe there is a God who created the universe, established the laws of science to govern the forces of nature and people, and then remains personally uninvolved. The complicated laws of nature run their course and God is the first cause of all of these laws, but God has not and will not intervene in how these laws affect the world. God never enters into the events of a person's life, nor a society's life.

In this view, God is like a master clock maker. The clock is made with all its intricate gears and mechanisms. It is wound up or plugged in and then the clock maker simply watches it work. No oiling, greasing or adjustments are necessary. It just keeps ticking.

According to the Deists, that's how God works. Once created, the universe is on its own.

We can very easily accept an active, personal God at home and in every setting except work and at the same time be inadvertent Deists at work. This dichotomy is possible when we don't really accept the varying degrees of Godpresence. Since our society "allows" God to be present in all settings except the workplace, it is easier to discover Godpresence in arenas other than work. However, since religion is not "allowed" in the workplace, we do not identify God as being truly present on the job.

But the fact that we have virtually eliminated God from the workplace doesn't mean that God has abandoned the workplace. Unfortunately, events and relationships which, outside of work, would be easily identified as obvious Godpresent events and relationships are not accepted with any reference to faith. Consequently, it is easy for us to become inadvertent Deists while at work.

As a result, those of us who wish to have an integrated faith life forget to focus on the active presence of God in the workplace. Our attention is drawn to more obvious areas of Godpresence—formal church settings, family, etc.—and to more intense Godpresent events. Godpresence on the job, therefore, is not identified, let alone accepted, nourished and celebrated.

As everywhere else, Godpresence at work is not just a matter of God hanging around watching us to see if we are doing good or evil. Godpresence, in any degree, is active. That activity can be summed up in one word: loving. As John said: God is love (1 Jn 4-8). God is at work and his job description is to love. But love is a complex and mysterious relationship which most of us have to break down into various parts in order to respond more effectively.

God's loving presence at and in work can be viewed from a number of perspectives. It's helpful to focus on two general characteristics of the Christian view of the loving God: God as creator and God as redeemer. God as creator relates to all those jobs whose essential task is to produce a product. God as redeemer relates to those jobs whose primary function is to offer a service. In some way, all work can be understood as either a product or a service. All work that produces a product, therefore, can more specifically relate to God as creator and all work that offers a service can more specifically relate to God as redeemer. Some products are also services, but the distinction between product and service is certainly acceptable.

God as Creator

Producing a product covers a wide range of work. From lawnmowers to balloons, automobiles to featherdusters, frying pans to cameras, frozen food to picture frames—every product made participates in God's original plan to create. Workers who produce products are co-creators with God. Workfaith makes it possible for us to recognize, understand and accept our role as co-creators while on the job.

God, of course, creates out of nothing. An act of God's will created the universe, regardless of the way the actual development of molecules took shape. The Big Bang theory may be correct, or the direct creation of galaxies, stars, and planets may be the actual historical event. In any case, the beginning of the universe and everything in it began with God creating by an act of divine will. Without God's creating, nothing would exist.

Continuing creation simply means that what was originally in existence continually takes on new forms and substances. Even believers who don't accept an evolutionary view of history admit that new forms, species and products come into existence. An evolutionist maintains that these new forms and species evolve out of previous substances and species. Combinations of chemicals, gases, or elements, aligned with atmospheric and other physical components, produce a new substance or species. Over time the world as it is now known came into existence.

The creationist version is that today's known world is the direct result of God's immediate creation. Evolution, they say, robs God of God's creative function, and attributes to humanity what can only be attributed to God.

In either view, we can identify with the creative role. We are not God; therefore, we cannot create out of nothing. We need something to start with before we can make something different out of the original materials. Granting that major limitation, it is legitimate to refer to us as co-creators in a theological sense. Those of us who work with our hands and/or our minds to produce a product, any product, are descendants of the original creative act initiated by God.

Because the production of many products is so complex, it takes many workers with many skills to turn out the final product. As a result, individual employees lose sight of their contribution to the ultimate product. We easily narrow our interpretation of our work to the specific task we do. American Airlines, where I work, has 100,000 employees around the world and, understandably, many departments with multiple functions to keep this company functioning.

We are in the airline transportation business and therefore we need a large reservation system, and marketing department along with personnel, maintenance, engineering, and accounting. We have pilots, flight attendants, mechanics, baggage handlers, ticket agents, computer experts, staff support personnel and thousands of other people with a great variety of titles and responsibilities. It is very easy for any of us to lose sight of the overall service we offer and to concentrate on our small piece of the corporate pie. Day to day details, hectic schedules, deadlines, local working conditions, co-wokers and job familiarity all contribute to the loss of overall perspective. I can be so occupied with my job that I can lose sight of the company's primary function. When I do that, I also lose sight of one of the main ways I have to relate my job to a product or service that ties in to God as creator and/or redeemer. Discovering God on the job becomes that much more difficult.

The fact remains that each and every one of us contributes to the production of a product or a service. For those who produce a product, it is helpful to recall that every product ever made is a continuation of the original act of God's creation. And every person who helped produce that product is a co-creator with God in the production of that product.

Workfaith makes it possible for us to recognize, understand and accept this connection between our work and our faith.

God as Redeemer

Those workers who are primarily in service work can relate, through workfaith, to God as redeemer. From the Christian perspective, God as redeemer requires a glance at God as Trinity and Jesus as human and divine.

The Trinity, Father–Son–Holy Spirit, is the Christian belief that there are three persons in one God. There are not three gods and there is not just one person. We believe that God has revealed the divine reality to be three persons in one

God. Centuries of debate has clarified but not diluted this fundamental belief.

The second person of the Trinity, the Son, has entered this world by becoming Jesus of Nazareth in order to offer redemption to a sinful humanity. All this is very basic and familiar to Christian believers. What is not so familiar is the connection between Jesus as redeemer and work that is service.

Service work includes all those functions and tasks that help other people. Manufacturing an automobile produces a product, but selling that same car is providing a service. Making lawn mowers is production, cutting the lawn is service. All marketing and selling is service because the product, presumably, does something for the customer. Some functions are obviously service: medical care, education, social services, government, military, etc. Workers are not always clear on whether we are in the product business or in the service business. And sometimes a job can be a little of both production and service. In any case, it is valuable to have a clear perspective on what business we are in at any given time so we can come to an understanding and acceptance of the value of our work.

Service workers can relate to Jesus as redeemer in a special way because redemption is the ultimate service offered to humanity. Redemption means that the purpose of creation can be fulfilled, even though humanity has sinned so severely that the original purpose could have been lost. Through Jesus' life, death and resurrection, redemption is accomplished. Participation in that redemption depends on personal faith, but the redemptive service of Jesus is the most basic, all-encompassing, significant service action ever performed. Jesus died and rose as a service to humanity. No other service goes that far or offers that much, with such fundamental consequences and such lasting benefits.

We who are service workers can deepen our understanding and broaden our acceptance of our daily labors when, through workfaith, we are able to connect our work with our faith in Jesus as redeemer. The service we offer is in the same general line or category as Jesus' service. Whenever a service, however trivial it appears, is offered, this service participates in the service that Jesus offered. The service of selling car insurance, for example, is certainly not the service of redemption. But selling car insurance is somewhat like redemption in that insurance offers some security and cushions the impact in case of an accident. Security and cushioning the consequences of an accident are somewhat like redemption in that redemption offers the greatest security of salvation and it certainly "cushions the impact" of sin. These similarities in words are not just semantics. Service workers can find comfort and challenge in workfaith which connects work with faith.

Trinity as Community

Another dimension to workfaith and Godpresence in the workplace is the Christian belief in the Trinity. The Trinity can be described as the perfect community. The three persons are distinct, yet they live together in community so closely that they are one nature. Through grace we share in that community to some extent here on earth. Participation in a faith community, and by extension, in any community is a small imitation of that perfect community that is Trinity. Salvation and heaven means that we share in that community to the fullest extent that human nature allows. Participation in that community in this world is at least one step removed from the heavenly participation, but nonetheless it is still participation.

Living in imperfect communities now, whether they be civic, religious, neighborhood, worldwide or workplace, are all imitations, in varying degrees of success, of that one perfect community that is the Trinity. Religious communities may make explicit references to this Trinity-participation and take specific actions to promote and foster this understanding and acceptance. But those communities, including secular workplace communities, that make no reference to the Trinity are still imitations of the Trinity and still participate to some degree in the Trinitarian community. In other words, all communities, whether they know it or not, are connected with the perfect community. This belief is simply another way of saying that all people, whether they know it or not, are connected with God. It just so happens that God is also a community.

Workfaith applies this general belief to the workplace. All workers are involved with other workers in some way or another. That makes working a community experience, and since Godpresence, in some degree or other, permeates the workplace, we can enrich our faith and our work by recognizing, understanding and accepting the connection between faith community and work community.

God as creator, Jesus as redeemer and the Trinity as community are three faith positions that underline the relationship between faith and work. Workfaith means to identify, uncover and support Godpresence at work, and to reject those forces that are contrary to Godpresence and gospel values.

Evil at Work

Evil in many forms is also present in the workplace. For now, it is enough to state that evilpresence and Godpresence, in fact, co-exist in many places, including the work arena. When the co-existence is identified in other areas of society—in the family, culture, public policy, etc.—the evil is often fought by concerned people. But when evil is identified in the workplace, it is either ignored or dealt with by the company or agency. Evil does not run wild in a particular workplace because the company is either fearful of lawsuits or genuinely wants to respect its employees and customers. It is simply good business to be fair and honest, to offer quality products and service. The fact that good business also coincides with Godpresence does not minimize the faith value of the business.

Evil does co-exist with Godpresence in the workplace. But that co-existence doesn't mean that God runs away from evil. The Holy Spirit does not shun a fight with evil. In fact, that's what Jesus and the cross and resurrection are all about. The Holy Spirit, who is today's active personal force showing us the way to Jesus who in turn takes us to the Father, struggles with and will eventually win over all evil. The struggle continues but the outcome is already determined: Jesus won the battle.

Evil remains because the final outcome has not yet permeated all of creation.

Too often we assume that the struggle between Godpresence and evilpresence in the workplace is not worth participating in from an explicit faith perspective. Or, if we do want to be an agent for supporting Godpresence and rejecting evil, we don't know how to do it. We are hampered because we cannot use God language to combat the evil. And since faith language is a major weapon in the struggle between good and evil in every part of life except work, we are confused and discouraged when we face evil at work. When we accomplish some good at work by changing an oppressive policy, increasing work productivity or improving employee respect, we don't associate this accomplishment with faith. And yet, these activities, which are always supported by the Holy Spirit even when we are not aware of it, may be our greatest contribution to gospel kingdom building. And since we aren't aware of it, we can't celebrate our work with the Spirit in extending God's kingdom in the workplace.

The worst work environment, then, does not mean that God is not present. The Holy Spirit is there, working to counteract evil and to foster love, but we don't recognize the Spirit because we can't see beyond the evil. Workfaith makes it possible to see the Spirit even when evil appears to dominate.

Workfaith: A Description

Workfaith is a term which, on the surface, simply combines the reality of work and the reality of faith. Most obviously it refers to the faith which we exercise when at work. Workfaith, more precisely, is not the faith which we bring to the job from other sources, like family, church, Bible study and prayer.

Believers with a fully integrated faith will be consistent in all areas of life, and can therefore speak of one, unified faith experience, regardless of where they are. Many of us, however, are not so integrated. Faith at work and faith at home can be very distinct, and at times contradictory. And even fully integrated believers will experience different aspects of faith in different settings. Faith at home may emphasize nurturing faith with children while faith at work may emphasize the co-creator role. In any case, workfaith refers to that faith which centers on the work experience.

A caution is in order. Faith, whether it be workfaith, home faith, church faith or social faith, is one in that it is a virtue within a single person. The person is fundamentally one, even though we may be functionally divided. Faith is personal knowledge of God. But this knowledge, and the trust that accompanies it, is not complete. Knowledge of God is necessarily limited, and we are always able to learn more about God. Centering on workfaith, then, is not intended to confuse us or divide faith into segments unnecessarily. Quite the contrary, workfaith is an effort to incorporate the work experience into a more integrated faith life and thereby offer an opportunity for greater knowledge of God. To accomplish this goal it is necessary to focus on faith at work, or workfaith.

There are legitimate distinctions between faith, morals and spirituality. These distinctions are valuable, and even necessary, since we are not able to assimilate everything at one time, nor are we able to make immediate connections among the many dimensions of our relationship with God. Faith, morality and spirituality each has a different, and valid, focal point when describing this relationship. Faith centers on knowledge and trust. The heart of morality is personal attitude, actions and behavior. Spirituality deals with the relationship between the human spirit and the Holy Spirit. All of these—faith, morality and spirituality—are ultimately united in a single believer. Growth in one area should imply growth in the other two areas, and often that seems to be the case. But we are not always consistent or logical and this parallel growth does not happen automatically.

Workfaith, as it is used here, attempts to incorporate faith, morality and spirituality. However, the primary focus is on faith, that is, on knowledge and trust. The contention is that the initial problem with uniting faith and work is the lack of knowledge and lack of trust that God is in fact an active, personal force (the Holy Spirit, to be precise) in and at work. The hope, however, is that this more accurate knowledge of Godpresence at work will lead to a more refined moral life as well as a more mature spiritual life.

Faith knowledge is more than just intellectual insight into God's revelation. Genuine faith is personal and it includes trust in the giver of the knowledge. In the case of workfaith, the personal presenter of this knowledge is God. Those of us who describe this knowledge and encourage this trust are mere channels of what God has already accomplished. We tell the story, as well and as accurately as we can. A preacher, theologian, teacher, or book cannot create faith in others. Faith is a gift from God alone. All that preachers, theologians, teachers or authors can do is point in a direction, with the invitation that if believers follow that direction, they may discover another aspect of God's revelation and thereby see God, through Jesus and in the power of the Holy Spirit, from another perspective. This new perspective may offer us the chance to deepen our faith, motivate our behavior and grow in our relationship with God. The role of pointing in the direction of revelation is the only role that anyone can have in terms of another person's relationship with God. In the final analysis, faith is personal, that is, it is between God and each believer.

Workfaith also implies knowledge of the specific requirements of the work activity. We need to understand the nature of the job we perform. Workfaith challenges us to find meaning in what we do not just in terms of getting a paycheck but also in terms of the work contributing to a product or service that has some value. If we see no value or meaning in the work

we do, we will not be able to experience workfaith in any significant degree. We bring meaning to our jobs but we must
also find meaning in the work itself. Workfaith opens the door
to understanding work as a contribution to building the kingdom of the creating and redeeming God. At this level, workfaith provides clarity and direction to the meaning of work.

Along with this understanding of work and faith comes
acceptance. Acceptance is an emotional attitude, the involve-
ment of the whole person in the work activity. To understand
workfaith is to possess some intellectual basis for the value of
work in the light of the kingdom and the gospel. To accept
workfaith is to commit emotionally to this value. We trust
that the work we do contributes to the kingdom. We accept
this reality as we accept the reality of the salvation offered by
Jesus. This knowledge and trust leads us to joy because we
are co-creating and serving in line with the call of the kingdom. This joy is probably not complete because the frustra-
tions, boredom, and values that are contrary to the kingdom
are also present. But workfaith can still usher in genuine
Christian joy because beyond all the negative experiences at
work, there is the underlying positive reality that the work
activity itself has creative and/or redemptive value.

We can recognize, understand and accept the value of
work in terms of personal faith. Making this connection is a
major step on the path to personal faith maturity and integration. Looking beyond ourselves, we can also recognize,
understand and accept our work in terms of building the
kingdom. We can participate with renewed enthusiasm in
those work functions which promote values consistent with
the kingdom. We know that we can make a difference and
we are dedicated to making that difference.

Finally, workfaith is used as one word in order to show the
intimate connection between work and faith. The perceived
division between these two realities has been so ingrained
that seeing them together in one word may appear shocking,
or, even worse, cute. The intention is not to shock and certain-

ly not to be cute. The intention is very serious: perhaps the visual use of this one word will reinforce a major and critical message.

God is present everywhere, and this Godpresence admits of varying degrees. But Godpresence can only be identified through faith. Workfaith is part of the equation as we focus on Godpresence in the workplace. God is at work, trying to be discovered, identified, supported and celebrated. Workfaith makes this discovery possible.

My Personal Journey

My personal journey into workfaith has led to peace and satisfaction at work and a renewed appreciation and gratitude for the redemption. Certainly there are still moments of stress and boredom, and I haven't discovered all the implications of workfaith in my own job. But I experience work today from a different perspective, a broader context.

When I recently moved into a new position, I felt the predictable anxiety of learning a new function and working with a different set of co-workers. After I got my desk in order, met some co-workers and understood in general terms what my new role would be, I took time to think and pray about this job from a workfaith point of view. What was my role and the role of this department in terms of the company? And what does this role and department have to do with faith? The answers are still coming but in general I was able to place this function within faith and kingdom building. We route aircraft for maintenance checks and we monitor aircraft maintenance performance. As such, we provide safety and security for our customers. We contribute to the kingdom because we make it possible for people to travel conveniently and meet with other people and/or places face to face. This growing personal contact with people and places contributes to the opportunity for greater communication and understanding among people. An overall sense of world oneness emerges. We help to "shrink the world" and thereby make the human community more knowledgeable about each other and hopefully more accepting.

Admittedly, flying to faraway places and meeting with people face to face may not generate immediate harmony among nations. Admittedly also, previous centuries did not provide easy access to faraway places and people, and all those people were likewise given the opportunity for salvation through the redemption earned by Jesus. But at this time, in this world, air travel is one method that is available for personal communication on a large scale. The village is now global. We are a service business that contributes to this global communication.

From a workfaith perspective, that's the broad context in which I go to work each day. While my piece of the pie is very small, at least I know what kind of pie we are. That awareness helps me appreciate and accept my job not only in terms of the work itself but also in terms of the relationship between my faith and my work.

My specific job task deals with gathering and distributing information regarding the schedule for aircraft maintenance. Each aircraft follows a detailed, precise maintenance program, and each aircraft is monitored daily. My work day can easily become a long list of phone calls, conferences, routing adjustments, reports, planning, and multiple meetings. Obviously, there are other people in the department who gather all this information and make hundreds of decisions to accomplish our tasks effectively and efficiently. Teamwork is essential.

All this activity can be included in workfaith. And for every piece of activity that I consciously incorporate into the broad picture I just outlined, I feel more at peace and more confident that what I do for eight to ten hours a day does, in fact, contribute to the kingdom as well as the performance of my company.

That's an overall description of how workfaith principles apply to my current job. I plan to fill in the picture in greater detail as time goes on, and I suspect that there will always be the need for more prayer and thought in order to appreciate the presence of God on my job. Undoubtedly, God as Trinity, and specifically Jesus as redeemer, is on the job with me. I need to turn on and tune in to that Godpresence more frequently and more clearly. And as I do, my faith will mature and my life will be more integrated. And I will be a happier person because my work life will be more closely connected with my faith life. I have begun this workfaith journey, and the benefits in understanding, discovery, awareness, peace, joy and commitment both to my job and to my God are remarkable. While this journey is not always easy, it is rewarding.

And I believe that all workers can start a similar journey, with similar results. In chapter 3 I will outline how ten different workers might apply these workfaith principles to their jobs. Hopefully, we will all make progress on a journey in which we continually discover, nurture and celebrate God on the job—including your job!

Study Questions

1. *Do you believe that God is present everywhere, even on your job? If so, does this belief make any difference?*

2. *In your own words, explain this position:*
   People who work in manufacturing jobs can relate more specifically to God's presence at work by reflecting on God as Creator and themselves as co-creators.

3. *In your own words, explain this position:*
   People who work in service jobs can relate more specifically to God's presence at work by reflecting on Jesus as Redeemer/Servant and themselves as servant/disciples of Jesus.

4. *What does the term "workfaith" mean to you?*

5. *How does viewing the Trinity as the Perfect Community help workfaith believers develop community at work?*

3

All Work Is God's Work

The word "work" must be overworked. According to the dictionary, work is an intransitive verb (to exert oneself in order to do or make something), a transitive verb (to bestow labor, toil, or exertion upon) or a noun (bodily or mental effort exerted to do or to make something). But that's only the beginning. The variations on these definitions take two large columns in a very large dictionary.

With all these possibilities, I have to identify the meaning of "work" here a little more precisely. In this context, the primary use of the word "work" is as a noun. Along with the "bodily or mental effort ..." definition, work is also described as "purposeful activity; labor; toil; employment; occupation; business; trade; craft; profession ..."

As the definition unfolds it implies that work is an activity we get paid for, although it could also be "bodily or mental effort" that does not earn money. In this broader sense, work includes housework, cutting the lawn, washing the car and homework, to mention only a few "bodily or mental efforts" most of us do without receiving a paycheck.

For our purposes, all of these work activities are included in workfaith. Some of us, for example, do housework because we want to live in a clean home and wear clean clothes. Other people do the same housework and get paid because it is their job. The core work activity is the same, and at this point the core work activity is the focal point. Therefore, whenever a reference is made to workfaith, the intention is to include home or hobby activities as well as compensated labor.

My examples and comments, however, will deal explicitly with those work activities that are commonly associated with a place of employment. This concentration is warranted because the problem with workfaith is most often identified with a job. The basic message applies to unpaid work activity as well as paid employment, but to avoid confusion and to deal with those aspects that *are* specific to a paid job, the primary context is the work exerted to pay the bills.

One more clarification is in order. Workfaith includes 1) the relationships with co-workers and 2) the core work activity itself. Many times the core work effort must be accomplished with co-workers; some jobs are necessarily communal. But even in these situations a distinction can be made between the work itself and the relationships with co-workers. For example, co-workers could dislike, undermine, and insult each other, but still work together because they have to in order to accomplish the task. The distinction, then, between relationships and work effort is an important one when considering workfaith.

This chapter centers on the work activity itself. Chapter 6 will consider relationships with co-workers. The topic of this chapter is one that many of us neglect when we reflect on faith at work. It is easier to make the connection between God's kingdom and work relationships than it is between the kingdom and specific work activity. What does any job have to do with building the kingdom? And most personally, how does my job and your job, the basic work we do every day, help build the kingdom? When I eliminate both my relationships with co-workers and what my earned money can do for me, what is left in regard to the kingdom?

At the end of chapter 2, I outlined some of the major workfaith themes that are related to my job. In this chapter I will describe the workfaith themes related to ten other jobs. The hope is that the workfaith perspective on these ten jobs will illustrate the approach and make it easier for all of us to follow a similar pattern in discovering Godpresence on our job.

The basic contention is that all work is ultimately connected to the kingdom, that is, each and every job does something that is in line with creation and/or redemption. Some work is relatively easy to identify as compatible with God's work. Other work seems a long way from the gospel. But regardless of how obvious or subtle the work is in terms of the kingdom, it remains true that all work is somehow God's work.

There is an immediate objection: What about drug dealers, murderers, prostitutes, muggers? What about workers whose intention is to steal, or gangsters, or people who make a product they know will harm others? Is this work also building the kingdom?

Those are the questions for the next chapter.

Here the intention is to establish the basic premise that all work is also God's work. This approach is to describe how ten different jobs could be understood as participating in building the kingdom. Five of these work activities are related to the theme of co-creator, and five are linked with the theme of service/redemption. Each job can be viewed from either the perspective of the work activity itself or from a broader outlook which includes the fact that each particular job contributes to the overall mission of a company or department.

Five Jobs Related to God as Creator

The following work activities are samples of manufacturing jobs, jobs which participate more specifically in building the kingdom of God because they are co-creative functions following the lead of the one and only creator God. There are many other manufacturing jobs, but the contention here is that a similar line of faith thinking can apply to them also. Ultimately, each of us will have to apply workfaith to our own jobs. Hopefully, these examples will offer some fresh insights into how to accomplish this task of integrating work and faith more effectively.

Pepsi Plant Workers

There's a story behind my choice of this job. Shortly after I started mulling over this topic of workfaith, I met with a small group of people from my church. It's a group that meets on Monday nights for prayer, scripture study and general faith discussion. Off and on, I had been a part of the group for many years and I knew everyone quite well.

On this particular night I wanted their reaction to my initial thoughts about workfaith. I knew they would be honest, and I figured they would be typical readers of a book like this. Their opinions were very important to me. I made a short presentation and distributed a brief hand-out. Their comments were very positive and they encouraged me to proceed. They easily identified with the problem—work and faith were not integrated very well in their lives either.

The problem was that parts of my evolving workfaith theme were not immediately clear to them. That's not surprising—they weren't all clear to me either! I asked for their suggestions. Ed raised the issue most explicitly: "You mean to tell me," he said skeptically, "that my neighbor who works at the Pepsi plant is contributing to the kingdom? That's hard to believe. Tell me how that's possible." Well, I said something about the value of all work and that "Yes, I believe your neighbor is contributing to the building of the kingdom." But Ed wasn't satisfied—and neither was I.

When I got home, I decided that the Pepsi plant worker was a personal challenge. So, I tried to understand the job from a workfaith perspective. I also figured I owed Ed a more complete response. Here's the way it looks to me now.

Let's begin with some questions: What value does a soft drink have to God? Does God care who drinks what brand of soft drink, or how it is made, or why it is made? Beyond the benefits of providing a paycheck for Ed's neighbor and other Pepsi workers and the relationships established in the plant, what value is there from God's point of view? How can believers be confident that working the second shift at our local Pepsi plant also contributes to the kingdom?

To answer these questions in any convincing way, we need to reflect on the purpose of the work activity. What does Pepsi do? Most fundamentally, Pepsi offers physical relief from thirst. That's what it is designed to do. Other products may relieve thirst better and be healthier, but in the final analysis Pepsi (and all other similar products) helps prevent suffering from thirst. In this sense, the basic product fulfills a corporal work of mercy and, as such, contributes to the building of the kingdom. The fact that employees of Pepsi may not understand or accept this dimension of their work illustrates that they haven't thought of this connection, but the reality remains that their work is inherently kingdom building.

Pepsi, of course, is in competition with many other drink producers. The fact that Pepsi spends a lot of money advertising its product in order to attract more drinkers does not eliminate the basic purpose of the product. The fact that the world doesn't have to have Pepsi in order to survive does not deny the reality that Pepsi does in fact quench thirst, at least to some degree. The fact that only people with a certain level of income can afford to buy Pepsi does not mean that the drink itself is less capable of quenching thirst. The fact that the company seems to ignore this basic benefit of its product in its advertising is probably due to the fact that stating it offers no competitive advantage over other similar products. In any case and despite all the advertised hype, Pepsi still fulfills its primary purpose: to give drink to the thirsty.

Is this insistence of the value of the fundamental function of Pepsi stretching it? Is this line of thinking too far-fetched to make any acceptable sense? Not at all! It is precisely this kind of reflection that opens the door to Godpresence at Pepsi plants in terms of the value of the specific work activity that takes place there. It is workfaith in action.

The problem is that many of us think an activity has to be more directly connected with biblical language and obvious "religious" products to be associated with building the kingdom. This approach states that making Bibles is kingdom enhancing but making Pepsi isn't. There's no question that some products, at first glance, are more obviously connected with the kingdom than other products. But what is obvious is certainly not the whole story. Actually, the point of workfaith (and any faith) is to see beyond the obvious and to discover the Godpresence in activities and areas where that presence is not yet accepted. God's activity is not limited to what we identify as obvious.

God is present in the process of producing Pepsi. People who assist in that process are working with God in making a product that quenches thirst. As such, these people are co-creators in the limited but real sense identified earlier. Workfaith believers at Pepsi are workers who understand and accept that their daily efforts, among other things, help produce a product that gives drink to the thirsty.

But isn't the kingdom a spiritual reality? Isn't the Holy Spirit only interested in people and their growth in holiness? How do worldly affairs like making Pepsi have anything to do with the kingdom?

It is true that the kingdom is within us. It is also true that the kingdom has an "outside" dimension to it. We are not just spirits who unfortunately happen to be encased in a body. We are body-spirit; our material makeup is an essential component of personhood. There is life after death, and this afterlife proceeds somehow without our physical bodies. How this next life, this "spiritual" life, functions is a mystery, but what we do know is that the next life is connected with this life. Spiritual does not mean anti-material. The next life means there is a new and different relationship between body and spirit, but there is a relationship. The spirit does not just discard the body as so much excess baggage. A relationship still exists between body and spirit.

Our belief in the resurrection of the body highlights that relationship. Just as we believe in the resurrection of Jesus' body and that his body is somehow with him in a spiritual state in heaven, so too all of us will have a relationship with our bodies in the next life.

The relevance of this reference to the body-spirit relationship both in this life and in the next is that, by extension, all matter, all things, are also part of the kingdom. Building the kingdom, then, is not limited to doing only "spiritual" things. That's why feeding the hungry, giving drink to the thirsty, clothing the naked and other works of mercy are accepted as building the kingdom. The line between spiritual and material is elusive because what is material has a spark of spiritual within it and what is spiritual is often encompassed in material.

Believers who work in a Pepsi plant (and any similar plant) can rest assured that their daily efforts are indeed contributing to the kingdom as they contribute to the production of a soft drink. They may feel that this contribution is minimal, that in the larger scope of things another case or truckload of Pepsi is not very significant. But it is precisely at this point that workfaith can be beneficial: each drop of Pepsi quenches a small need for liquid. The kingdom is built by small acts and, occasionally, by a very large, obvious event. But most of the time, kingdom building is comprised of small, seemingly insignificant acts and events. At the end, at the second coming of Christ, everyone will be aware of how the kingdom was created and how it grew. And we will be amazed at how much the kingdom was built by seemingly small, insignificant acts and events, many of them taking place on the job.

There are also other avenues of reflection that Pepsi plant workers could pursue in order to clarify the value of workfaith. At times, Pepsi contributes to a social event, providing a leisure time drink that aids in the building of community. All communities, as was mentioned earlier, are an imitation of the perfect community, the Trinity. At times, the Pepsi company may sponsor an event which helps build community. The company may also discover ways to make Pepsi that improve the working conditions of the employees as well as increase productivity and quality. In any case, while the main function of making Pepsi, from the perspective of workfaith, is to participate in the creative process, it is likely that believers in a Pepsi plant will discover other ways in which their product helps build the kingdom. It is precisely this kind of reflection that will assist believers in integrating work and faith.

Obviously, the variety of workers at a Pepsi plant perform a variety of functions. Assembly line workers have different job descriptions than office staff or maintenance, and management has another set of daily duties. Each of these divergent job responsibilities has its own specific contribution to the overall product, and believers in each of these areas will have to identify in greater detail the contribution they make both to producing Pepsi and to building the kingdom. But to understand and accept their role as co-creators with God in producing a product that gives drink to the thirsty is a good starting point for believers who want to integrate work and faith.

Most of these comments, of course, are not limited to believers who work in a Pepsi plant. Most of these observations can be made of all products, once the basic connection between God as creator and the manufactured product is made. The contention here is that this connection can always be made.

I mentioned this fuller explanation of workfaith as it might apply to his neighbor, and Ed seemed more satisfied. He's still thinking about it, but he now accepts the basic approach. Knowing Ed as I do, I consider that a major breakthrough!

Photographers

A friend of mine has a daughter who is a professional photographer. She does portraits as well as fashion shots for catalogues and occasionally for magazines. I am a very lousy photographer and, fortunately, confine my attempts at photography to family vacations when I hope to capture enough of the mountains or ocean or whatever, along with the appropriate family member, to remind us of the wonderful vacation we had. My faltering efforts make me appreciate good photographers. This also makes me want to look at the workfaith dimension of photography.

The job of a freelance photographer may be interpreted as a service or as a product. Any number of jobs have this double interpretation. In a situation like this, from the point of view of workfaith, it is important to zero in on one interpretation at a time. On the other hand, freelance photographers have the advantage of recognizing, understanding and accepting the connection between work and faith from at least two perspectives.

The comments here will consider photography as a product, that is, a picture has been developed. The content of the photograph is, for the most part, irrelevant. In other words, for our purposes, a photograph of a church or a pastor isn't any more religious than a picture of the family at Grand Canyon or little Jimmy swinging at a whiffle ball. In terms of a product, a picture is a picture.

What actually do we do when we take a picture? We freeze a moment. The picture stops time and records what went on during that brief millisecond. (Video cameras capture ongoing movement, but they essentially do the same thing: they preserve one event so it can be repeated during a succeeding event.) Whether that one moment is joy-filled, like a birthday celebration, or tragic, like the devastation from a hurricane, the essential work activity remains the same. Photographers, both professional and amateur, play with time. We attempt to rearrange the sequence of events. What was "before" becomes "now."

Obviously, this transposition of time is not complete or perfect. The event recorded on film really happened only during the original experience. However, the picture, when viewed later, is an imitation of the original event. The photograph doesn't capture the whole experience—feelings, circumstances, what led up to that one transposed millisecond and what followed it, are not recorded. But for that one split second, time is frozen.

In creating the universe, God created time and space. Space means that everything has to be somewhere. Time means that there is always a "before" and an "after." Those two realities of space and time are essential to this universe; everything everywhere is touched by space and time.

But the creator was looking beyond the universe to the "next" life, the life of heaven, the life when all creation will manifest the will of the creator and all people will know the love of God and the communion of saints—and when all people will no longer be confined to space and time.

Among other things, heaven means there is no time. All events are a perpetual "now"; God's love and the heavenly believers' response to that love is a constant, never-changing, always current happening. The eternal "now" destroys "before" and "after."

In a very limited but real way, a picture imitates this timelessness of heaven. Photographers touch timelessness. And in doing so, they touch the final purpose of creation. A picture attempts to change a "before" into a "now," a continuing "now." The fact that this freezing of time is not perfect does not minimize the extent to which this manipulation of time succeeds. To a large degree, a photograph does capture time and moves a "before" into a "now." To that degree, it also makes eternity current.

Workfaith can add another dimension to the work of photographers by placing this work in the context of a creation encased in time and space, but aiming at the timelessness of the final and complete fulfillment in God.

Undoubtedly, other workfaith dimensions for photographers are also possible. When photographers focus on workfaith, we will surely discover many ways in which God is present in this profession. We simply need to look at our experience in the light provided by the Holy Spirit and the guidance given by the church, and we will find a richness in this work that we never imagined.

Children's Toy Makers

There are many manufacturing jobs. In some way each of them is related to the creative function. The task of workfaith believers is to identify that connection, meditate on it and let that belief enter into their work experience.

A few more examples of this relationship between faith and specific work activities will be helpful. A brief analysis of children's toy making will demonstrate another dimension to the workfaith process. Why toy making? Because it seemed more difficult to relate to workfaith than making cars, refrigerators or furniture, and because toy making appears to be more frivolous, and therefore less obviously kingdom building, than other manufacturing jobs.

How does the job of making toys contribute to the building of the kingdom? The first step in answering this question is to state the nature of the work activity in its most simple and most basic form. What is it that this job produces? The answer to this question can be stated in a variety of ways. What is important is that the answer is relatively accurate.

One answer in regard to toy makers is that toys help children have fun. That's one accurate answer. And if the core value of toys is to entertain children, that entertainment can also be related to the kingdom. Experiencing joy because of a toy is a brief imitation of the joy intended for us both in this life and in the next. All joy participates in God's joy—certainly in a limited way but nonetheless in a real way. Workfaith believers who are toy makers can center on this aspect alone and discover God's creative presence in their work.

But other dimensions are also possible. Along with fun, children can develop social, physical and mental skills by playing with toys. A specific toy is not the only way to develop these skills but in fact specific toys do contribute to these skills. Obviously some toys are better at teaching these skills but, in some way, all toys do something for children that goes beyond just fun. Interaction with other children, motor skills, creative game development and intellectual curiosity are just a few of the possible benefits of playing with toys.

These benefits can be gained without the use of specific toys. Children have a tendency to make their own toys when they don't receive them. A rock, a stick, a pile of dirt all become "toys." But this reality doesn't undermine the benefits of the many toys produced by toy makers. Does the world need all these toys? No! But, again, the multitude of toys doesn't eliminate the value of each of them.

But what does this product, in this case this toy, have to do with God's kingdom? In the case of toys, one connection with the kingdom centers on the creation of community. Toys can be an excellent way in which children learn to socialize. The better they become at this skill the closer they are to the kind of social skills needed for the faith community and ultimately for heaven. There's a major difference between a four year old riding a bicycle with a neighbor and the social life of the communion of saints. But there is also a connection—the initial socializing of the bicycle riders is pointed in the direction of the final, glorified community. God's presence to the little riders invites them in that direction, perhaps slowly and imperceptibly, but also inevitably.

Bicycle makers can find some encouragement in this line of thinking. Their bicycles provide many benefits for children—and each benefit can be tied to some aspect of community, some skill or some positive experience associated with the bicycle. Just because people have not identified these benefits as connected with the kingdom doesn't mean that they are not connected.

But suppose some toy makers are not at all interested in the benefits of their toys for children. Suppose the only thing these toy makers are interested in is their paycheck. Everything else is totally irrelevant to them. These workers will not benefit from workfaith but, regardless of their attitude, they still produce products that provide entertainment and develop skills for children. In this minimal sense, they inadvertently

contribute to the kingdom. It takes faith to recognize and celebrate this connection between work and faith, but, even
unrecognized, God's presence has power.

Toy makers, and other manufacturers, have different job
responsibilities. Those workers who run the drill presses, for
example, have different work experiences from those who sit
behind a desk. They all contribute to toy making (or whatever
the product is), and in that sense they can all share in a similar
workfaith perspective in terms of the product they all produce. But they can also look more closely at their individual
jobs. Drill press operators, for example, can think of their
machine as an extension of their hands. These operators physically shape some raw material, some elements into a different
shape and a different product. From a workfaith viewpoint,
they are exercising dominion over the earth (Gn 1:28). They
are co-creating with God in the sense that they are rearranging
God's elements in order to produce something different.

Those of us who sit behind a desk can take a different
approach. We develop and maintain procedures that make the
production run smoothly—we plan, organize resources, manage the paperwork, implement each step to guarantee a final
product, pay the bills and evaluate the whole process.
Workfaith helps us see the connection between our work and
faith, perhaps in the context of the first book of Genesis
which begins with a reference to bringing "order out of
chaos." Without the work of us desksitters, toy production
would be chaos—and soon there would be no production. We
are co-creators in the sense that we imitate God's creation by
bringing order out of chaos.

Various work groups, then, can find their own specific
application of workfaith to accompany the workfaith value of
the product the company produces.

With prayer, thought and some discussion, believers who are
toy makers will discover other ways to connect their basic work
with God's kingdom. The connection is there because God is
there. It's up to believers to identify and magnify that presence.

Boxmakers

Many of the previous comments about Pepsi plant workers, photographers and toy makers also apply to box makers—and many other work activities. For workfaith to be specific and personal, however, it is necessary to identify some particular connection between work and faith for each job or each product.

I chose box makers because of my wife. The husband of one of her co-workers works at a place that makes boxes. He feels that his job is meaningless, routine and offers no challenge. His dissatisfaction is great and he is looking for another job. But until then, he has to "put up with" working in the box plant.

In some ways, he is not unlike many other workers. If the reports are true, most people are dissatisfied with their current job, and stay with it only because they figure they don't have other alternatives. In any case, because of this man's dissatisfaction with his job, I decided to try to discover a workfaith dimension to box making in the hope that other people with similar feelings might find some encouraging dimension to their present job.

The first step in clarifying the workfaith dimension of any job is to state the nature of the job in simple and basic terms. What does this work activity do or provide? Box makers, for example, produce containers designed to hold things. Boxes make it possible to move or store quantities of items efficiently and protect them from damage during shipping. Without boxes, moving items would be much more difficult and many more things would be broken.

Box makers are in the protection and transportation business.

One workfaith connection for box makers is to reflect on this protection in the light of creation. God is the ultimate Creator of all things, even if people have shaped and reshaped certain raw materials into many various products. Most boxes, for example, began as trees. Trees are a product of nature, and God is the author of nature. The purpose of boxes is to protect other items that can trace their history to God. Boxes keep things from being lost or destroyed (or, at least, reshaped!) and in so doing they are co-creative in that they are preserving the shape of items that may be fashioned by people but which have their ultimate source in God. Box makers are the protectors of a piece of this created universe. They are co-creators in that they preserve manufactured products which in the final analysis have their origin in God.

This theme of protection can be traced back to the Genesis account of God granting people "dominion over the fish of the sea, the birds of the air, and all the living things that move on the earth" (Gn 1:28). To receive the right, responsibility, obligation and privilege to have "dominion" is truly awesome. It implies respect for the things and creatures of this earth, decisions that honor the nature of each being, attitudes that foster harmony among all things and species, policies that promote understanding and acceptance of the inherent dignity of each creature and each object, and actions that reflect God's care and concern for the whole created world. Dominion is not dominance. Domination destroys; dominion nurtures, protects, and guides all things toward their ultimate end: union with God.

That is the broad workfaith context in which a box maker labors. The individual tasks of making, shaping and distributing boxes all participate in this grand vision of God's creation and cosmic harmony. Through the eyes of workfaith, a box maker can discover greater meaning in seemingly insignificant, routine and boring tasks.

Is this analysis making more out of a job than is really there? After all, a box is a box. No, it is not exaggerating! It is simply attempting to identify the Godpresence that is already active in the work. Is this reflection the only and final analysis of Godpresence in box making? Certainly not! Box makers who are believers could undoubtedly find other connections between their work and God. They simply have to be pointed in that direction and given "permission" to identify the creator God who is present to them in and at work.

Television Manufacturers

We all watch television. Some of us probably watch too much but in any case television has rapidly moved to the center of our entertainment, information and cultural life. That's why I chose television manufacturers as the final example of people who produce products and who, therefore, can find a workfaith connection between their job and God as creator.

The focus here is on the making of televisions, not the producing of television programs. Television programming relates more directly to service in that the intention of the programs is to entertain and/or to educate. Television manufacturing relates more to creation in that the production process continues the creative momentum initiated by the creator.

What do TV makers actually do? Here is one answer: they harness and direct the laws of physics in order to produce a visual and audio image of something or someone who is not present. The laws of physics, and in general the laws of nature, were originally established by the creator, regardless of whether they were directly created by God or whether they evolved by the interaction of gases, elements, compounds, atmospheric conditions and human manipulation. The source is ultimately God alone.

People who discover and work with these laws of nature are cooperating with the creator in applying these laws to specific purposes. It is an easy next step to claim that these people are co-creators with God because they work with and shape these laws by bringing out their inherent qualities and producing useful products which enhance the living experience of society. The fact that some of these applications can be harmful does not mean that the process of producing these products is harmful. We can choose to misuse anything. This misuse doesn't negate the co-creative value of the basic process.

TV manufacturers, then, use the laws of physics to make their televisions. Just as the photographers mentioned earlier tamper with time by making the past "present," so too television makers tamper with both time and space. A television image transfers an event that took place at a given time in a given space and makes that event available at a different time and space. Even though the original event may have been "staged," that staged program is transferred from one place to other places by means of video/audio images. If the event is "live" television, then the TV manipulates space. If the program is pre-recorded, then the TV manipulates both space and time. In either case, television manufacturers, and other manufacturers who use the laws of nature, are working with God, whether they know it or not, in applying these laws to the production of their products.

This line of thinking can open the doors to on-the-job kingdom building for many believers who manufacture products. Other workfaith ramifications are certainly possible, and believers who want to integrate their faith and their work more extensively will discover these connections.

Five Jobs Related to God
as Redeemer–Servant

The second category of work activity is service. Many jobs are some form of service. All stores are service based; selling, in general, is a service job. Education, health care, insurance, government agencies, military operations and food distribution are just some of the more obvious service related professions. In fact, it's commonplace today to hear social analysts claim that the United States has more people employed in the service sector than in the manufacturing sector. Whether that claim is true or not, it is certainly true that there are many people who do work in service jobs.

Some work is both manufacturing and service. For example, contractors who build homes are both producing a product (a home) and providing a service (the same home). From a workfaith perspective, both of these avenues of reflection can be beneficial. Workfaith believers simply have to look at one or the other, or both possibilities, in order to discover the God who is already present in the home building process.

My own job history has been service oriented. Priest, teacher, education director, training and operations manager are all essentially service positions. I have tried to help people learn things about themselves, God, community, and, currently, aircraft. I have dealt with information from the Bible, church teaching, theologians and "experts" as well as information from our company policies and procedures. I gather information and I disseminate information and, as such, I am a servant. While the specifics of my work history is somewhat unique, and covers a diversified spectrum, it is, and always has been, a work of service. At that very basic level, my work is similar to the work of millions of other servants who have thousands of different jobs and thousands of different work situations. But we all remain servants. How well we serve is another issue. The fact remains: when we work, we serve.

In general, the relationship between service work and kingdom building centers on Jesus, the redeemer/servant. Christians believe that Jesus, both divine and human, entered this world in order to redeem this world. The world is in need of redemption because we are sinners who turned away from the inherent purpose of creation by freely choosing selfishness and pride over love and humility. Humanity is so tainted by this diversion that the path to the ultimate goal of life was fundamentally blocked. But the God who is Trinity did not abandon the people who abandoned God. The Trinity choose to send the second person to the world in order to demonstrate the extent of God's love. Jesus of Nazareth is that second person, or Son, and this same Jesus is also completely human.

Jesus therefore bridges the gap between God and humanity because Jesus is both God and human. He was identified and accepted as human by his contemporaries, and he experienced the joys and sorrows of human life. His mission of redemption took him to the limits of life, namely to death. His suffering, passion and death dramatized the unconditional and limitless love God has for creation, and in particular for the highlight of creation—humans. Jesus restated this love in very human terms so people wouldn't miss it again or misinterpret or ignore it. The death and resurrection process offers hope and salvation for all of us and is the cornerstone of Christian faith. Christians are people who got the message of God's love most clearly and who try to live in response to that love. Other people may get the message in other ways, but we believe that the clearest and most direct message of God's love is found in Jesus of Nazareth.

Among other appropriate titles, servant is certainly applicable to Jesus. What he taught and what he did, not only in his death and resurrection, but also throughout his life, is imbued with service. He was constantly serving the sick, the troubled, and the confused. His mission was fundamentally to serve a sinful world by offering salvation. There is no service greater than making it possible for people to enjoy God's love eternally. No service is as significant or unique.

However, God choose to communicate this unconditional love in very human terms. God normally does not show this redemptive service through spectacular, extraordinary events. Respecting our humanity, God offers this redemption through Jesus in ways that are compatible with human intellect, free will and emotions. We "see" this redemptive service in the experiences of our lives, in sacraments, prayer, other people, nature and even within ourselves.

Jesus also challenged his followers to be funnels of God's love to others. By our faith, hope and love, we are witnesses to Jesus and to God's service to humanity.

The kingdom of God on earth grows as the redemptive service of Jesus extends and manifests itself throughout the world. Through the activity of the Holy Spirit, the redemptive service of Jesus permeates the world.

The Holy Spirit works in ways that are mysterious to us. We

see traces of Spirit-work in formal religious settings and in surprising personal experiences. As we learn to recognize this Spirit-work through faith, we understand and accept Godpresence more intensely.

We who are service workers can relate to this redemptive service of Jesus. All Christians, of course, will accept this mission and ministry of Jesus. But we who are also employed in service positions can integrate our work and our faith by recognizing, understanding and accepting the redeemer/servant theme as it applies to our daily work.

This outline of the general theological basis of workfaith as it applies to service work provides a backdrop for the following examples of the integration of service work and faith. As you read these examples, apply them to your own work experience.

Counselor

My first example is personal. My wife is a drug and alcohol counselor, and so we are familiar with the counseling profession. She too wants to integrate work and faith in her life; choosing counseling, then, as an example of service work is a "natural." Besides, it gives me an in-house expert to check my ideas.

Counselors offer service to people who have needs they can't resolve themselves. There are, of course, many kinds of counselors; academic, family, spiritual, physical, emotional, and, of course, drug and alcohol are just a few. What these various positions have in common is that they make it possible for clients to discover insights about themselves, or possibilities they haven't considered, which help them cope with life more successfully. Family counselors, for example, may assist families in identifying destructive behavior or attitudes and then help these families develop healthier ways to relate. This assistance is clearly a service.

The effectiveness of this service may be questionable. Some families may be very responsive while other families can't seem to make any significant changes in their destructive patterns. For success, therefore, counselors must depend on the willingness and ability of the clients to make some changes in their lives. If there is resistance to these necessary changes, even the best counselors will probably not succeed.

The same reality is true of academic counselors. Our twins are now beginning their senior year in high school. The decisions about college: what kind of college, where, what is the right major, what is the cost, what does it lead to, who makes what decision—we are in the middle of these decisions. Academic counselors, both at the high school and from different colleges, are extremely important to us right now.

These counselors may develop excellent education plans and give us valid information regarding study habits, for example, but if our twins (and any student) are not motivated or become distracted or are not committed enough, the plans will not work.

Counselors, then, depend on clients to be successful.

Therefore, even though it is relatively easy to identify the role of counselors as servants and then to connect this profession with redemptive service of Jesus, it is necessary to identify this relationship a little more specifically.

Like counselors, Jesus too depends on people to respond. He asks for faith. We can choose to reject that offer. Jesus has in fact earned redemption for all of us but each of us has to accept that salvation. Jesus respects human freedom so much that he doesn't force himself on anyone.

Counselors can relate to this aspect of Jesus' service. Good counselors don't force themselves or their ideas on others. Good counselors respect the freedom of their clients even as the counselors help the clients discover better ways to live. Counselors may know very well what the clients need to do to live more effectively, and they may even help the clients discover what is wrong and what the necessary steps are to improve. This assistance, however, is not enough. Frustration can set in for counselors because, in the final analysis, the clients can choose whether they will make the necessary changes or not.

Workfaith counselors may find it consoling and encouraging to identify with similar experiences of Jesus who consistently pointed the way to a better life and who consistently was ignored. The consolation comes not only from this identification but also from the fact that Jesus ultimately does have the answer to life. In other words, even though counselors experience some failures, they can be encouraged by the belief and the confidence that their service is helpful to some people, if not all people.

Counseling, and professions like it (teaching, medical care, coaching, etc.), are rich in possibilities in regard to workfaith. The primary and critical step is to convince counselors, and other similar service workers, that they are in fact contributing to the kingdom, even though they never make a reference to God or Jesus. "Secular" counselors, teachers, doctors, etc. also help people. It's the helping that benefits the kingdom, not just the Christian label.

On the other hand, explicit references to the kingdom, God, Jesus and church make the connection between work and faith much clearer. In those environments where explicit use of faith language and activity are possible, the clients or students or patients have the opportunity to witness the relationship between service and God very directly. In many cases, these explicit references to God make it easier for counselors to understand and accept the relationship between their work and their faith.

The point here, however, is that this relationship also exists when there is no specific reference to God or faith. This relationship exists in varying degrees, even though some counselors ignore it or deny it. Helping others is automatically a part of kingdom building.

Electricians

Another, but very different, service is the work of an electrician. Electricians, most simply, install or repair electrical systems in order to make electricity available. It is a profession that is obviously a service, and therefore workfaith electricians can connect their work with their faith by reflecting on Jesus as redeemer/servant.

Workfaith for electricians can be more enriching, however, if they are able to make this connection more precisely.

Most of us take electricity for granted. We turn on a switch and the light goes on. We pop in some bread and out comes toast. We turn the key and the car starts. Most of us, I dare say, know little about the physics of electricity. If we studied it in high school, we forgot most of it. What we do know is that we are afraid of electricity—I certainly don't want a jolt of that stuff, in any dosage! But despite our ignorance and fear, electricity makes life as we know it function. Without it, life would be very different.

Obviously, other societies are possible. Humanity got along without electricity for many centuries, so it is not absolutely necessary for survival. On the other hand, society as it has developed is now dependent on electricity. It is so interwoven into current life styles that removing it would mean dramatic adjustments. Many people would have severe difficulties making these adjustments. Housing and lighting would have to be completely changed. There would be no appliances. Electrical systems that pump water would not be available. Artificial air conditioning would be non-existent. Aircraft, automobiles, buses and trucks would be fantasies. The list goes on and on. Imagine life two centuries ago. Those are the kinds of changes that would be made if electricity had not been harnessed.

Some of you may argue that living the life style of two centuries ago would be an improvement over current experiences. Be that as it may, electricians still provide a necessary service to this society.

Does God really care if we have electricity? Does it make any difference to God that electricians install and repair electrical systems? Isn't God really interested only in relationships among people, regardless of whether it's an "electrical society" or a cave dwelling society?

God is primarily interested in people. But God never deals with people in isolation. God seems to accept people in whatever the culture happens to be. The Old and New Testaments demonstrate over and over again that God works within the current society. Jesus, for example, never attempted to "modernize" Jewish society. He accepted it as it was, that is, he never attempted to throw the Romans out or change the local currency or even reject normal customs. He did attempt to change people, to convert them to a new way of faith, hope and love. He was a social reformer in the sense that society needed to reflect more accurately the principles of the kingdom, namely to love God and neighbor. These principles would radically alter society in the sense that relationships and institutions would have to change fundamentally.

But Jesus didn't care whether a house was lit with a brand name oil bought at Neiman Marcus or a different oil from the local Wal-Mart. He didn't care whether a road was paved or dirt, or how shepherds worked with the sheep, or how fishermen caught fish, or what label was inside a toga. He accepted society as it was, except where it interfered with the kingdom and his mission. God, therefore, works with societies that have electricity and with societies that don't have it.

But God takes people, and their society, where they are. Typically, all societies have forces that support and forces that minimize the kingdom. In itself, electricity neither supports nor rejects the kingdom.

However, the elimination of electricity in our society would cause havoc, and God does care about havoc. There is no evidence that God is opposed to the technological advances modern society has spawned—as long as they don't interfere with the kingdom. In fact, a case can be made that many of these advances, including electricity, do support the kingdom. They improve communications which provide opportunities to develop a global community which could more closely imitate the perfect community, i.e. the Trinity.

The friendly electrician, then (and he was friendly!), who

came to connect the pump for the French drain we had to install recently is contributing to the kingdom. This project keeps water from entering the air duct system in our home. Without it we run the risk of mildew, increased allergies and a rapidly deteriorating heat and air conditioning system. The electrician provided a service that helps make our family and home more liveable. In itself, that work is kingdom building.

Electricity is a force of nature that is controlled and put to use by electricians. These workers channel the laws of nature into specific useful functions. They help us use nature. They are servants who imitate Jesus, the servant. They may not know it, and they may even deny it, but the workfaith reality is that their service participates in the great service of redemption that Jesus accomplished. Since God is everywhere and since Jesus, the redeemer/servant, is God, Jesus too is everywhere as redeemer/servant. Any service, anywhere, whether small or large, shares in and reflects that basic, all-pervasive service of Jesus.

Aircraft Mechanic

Since I work for the maintenance division of an airline, I just had to include aircraft mechanic in this list of service occupations. I am not an aviation technician (the more accurate and official FAA title for what is commonly called an airplane mechanic). I personally do not maintain aircraft. But I work with a lot of people who do, and with my growing familiarity with their knowledge, skill and dedication, I am even more impressed and inspired with their ability and the service they provide.

Basically, their work is preventive maintenance. Their primary task is to keep the aircraft flying so efficiently that the planes never crash. They also must maintain passenger "convenience" items: coffee makers, reading lights, air conditioning systems, seat adjustments, tray tables, etc. As service professionals, these aviation technicians automatically reflect the basic service of redemption that Jesus accomplished.

There are a number of ways aircraft mechanics can make the connection between their work and their faith. In a broad sense, airlines bring people together, whether for business, vacation, family reunions, or visits between friends. Passengers arrive at destinations considerable faster than through other means of transportation. In many cases, the faster travel makes the trip possible, and long distance travel would be greatly reduced without air service.

Air transportation provides opportunities for more people to meet face to face and to see places they would never have visited. This accelerated communication and personal familiarity with places makes it more possible for the world community to become a better community. There is no guarantee that frequent travel by greater numbers of people will build a better world, but there is a good possibility that tolerance, acceptance, understanding and support will increase when people know one another better.

The airline industry, then, provides a service which contributes to the building of community, and, as been noted, all communities mirror the communitarian life of the Trinity. Airline mechanics can legitimately connect their work with their faith by reflecting on this theme.

These technicians can also pursue another theme. Their work is basically preventive maintenance. All their skills and tasks are directed toward preventing maintenance problems. This emphasis on prevention is something like Jesus, the servant, urging his followers to avoid sin, to stay away from those circumstances which may distract them from the goals of the kingdom. In the Sermon on the Mount, for example, Jesus constantly warns his listeners of the dangers of pride, wealth and selfishness (Mt 5). He wants to warn and protect his disciples from these traps.

In somewhat the same way, aviation technicians serve the flying public by protecting them from possible maintenance failures. Mechanics can relate to Jesus the servant through the work they do because of this inherent relationship to prevention. Jesus of course deals with the greatest dangers people face—sin, pride and selfishness. But these technicians, and many similar professionals, deal with potential disaster on a daily basis. Mechanics can find consolation, strength and a personal identification with Jesus in this mutual interest in preventing disasters.

With this perspective, aviation technicians will listen to the gospel and discover many similarities between their faith and their work. Workfaith believers are people who read the gospels, pray in private and in the liturgy—all from the viewpoint of their work. We ask ourselves: what is it that I do at work each day? Then we ask: what does my basic work activity have to do with God, as revealed in the scriptures and as present to me as creator and redeemer/servant? Different people will come up with different passages or themes that are relevant to them. That diversity is to be expected—and enjoyed. What is most important is that we do in fact make the connection between work and faith.

Computer Specialists

The job of computer specialist offers a different approach to connecting work with faith. Computers are extensions of the human mind just as screwdrivers are an extension of the human hand. Since the mind is much more complex than the hand, so too computers are more complex than the screwdriver. Computers collect, organize, sort and distribute information at incredible speeds and accuracy. They make it possible to analyze data more thoroughly than most of us ever could. They process and deliver an amazing amount of information in a multitude of formats, styles and depth. As a result they make it possible for us to make more informed and, presumably, better decisions.

By computer specialists I mean those people who Know Stuff About Computers. What stuff? I don't know! All that stuff about how computers work, how they can be programmed, what hard drives go with what, when a mainframe is better than a personal computer, what megabytes are needed for a specific function, what boards are needed, etc., etc. By computer specialist I am not talking about people like me, people who can use a word processor or speadsheet program just well enough to benefit from its basic features. The specialists go way beyond our knowledge and ability.

Computer specialists are servants in that they manipulate computers and all the information they provide. Since computers are an extension of our minds, these specialists work with functions and programs that emulate certain mental capabilities. These specialists serve people by designing, developing, and maintaining computers which increase knowledge, analyze data, improve productivity (e.g. word processing), and identify relationships between different bodies of information. Many of these functions could be done by some people. Most of us, however, couldn't do them at all, in terms of either speed or accuracy.

Workfaith believers who are computer specialists can relate to Jesus the redeemer/servant by reflecting on the many times Jesus challenged the thinking and stretched the minds of both his followers and persecutors. For example, the title "messiah" had a definite cultural meaning among the Jews at the time of Jesus. The expected messiah would drive the Romans out of the country and bring peace and prosperity to the Israelites. These popular connotations were a distortion of the original meaning but, nonetheless, they were embedded in the minds of the people. Jesus, therefore, had to change their thinking about the meaning of the word messiah as he revealed to them that he was the messiah. Jesus was trying to extend the thinking of his listeners and in doing so to offer them a service, that is, to know him as the true messiah. Computer specialists may find some familiarity with this aspect of Jesus in that they too try to extend our thinking and provide new information and new ways to look at things.

Jesus also serves the human mind by revealing his relationship with the Father. In itself, this belief in the divinity of

Jesus is information. We accept this information on faith; we believe that Jesus claimed divinity and we accept him as trustworthy. With this knowledge we interpret reality, and the world, God and people make some sense. This revealed information is the basis for ultimate meaning in life. Without this knowledge, reality loses its center and disintegrates into countless bits of unrelated experiences and events.

The information provided by computer specialists is certainly not as critical as belief in the divinity of Jesus. In fact, information gained by faith and information gained by reason (including computer generated information) are essentially different processes. But faith and reason are not contradictory. A faith position can also be reasonable, at least up to the point of not being unreasonable. By the same token, reason can come to some conclusions about God, e.g. the probable existence of a God. In any case, faith and reason, while very different in how they produce data, are similar in that they do present information. That similarity can be a source of insight for workfaith believers who are computer specialists.

Once again, these workfaith believers will undoubtedly find many connections between their megabytes, video boards, RAM of memory, chips and other assorted mysteries, and their belief in Jesus as redeemer/servant. High tech industries in general can reflect the marvelous wonders of God and especially how God, in Jesus, channels the greatest of these wonders into the service of redemption. Computer specialists, like many similar professionals, have many opportunities for workfaith.

Secretaries

From a workfaith perspective, secretaries can relate to God as creator and Jesus as redeemer/servant. One reference to God as creator has already been made: people who work behind desks in administrative functions attempt to bring order out of chaos. That characterization is surely true of the role of secretary.

Another workfaith approach revolves around the role of secretary, or administrative assistant, as servant. Most of the secretaries that I have had or know object to the title and implications of the word "servant." They perceive the term as demeaning. They will be forced to bend their will to others. Being a servant is not equated with slavery, but the core of their servant's relationship to a boss or company owner is functionally one of an inferior to a superior. Even in the best of situations, even when people treat each other with mutual respect, the essential role of the servant is to do things for other people. Many of the secretaries I know resent this aspect of their job.

Many jobs fit into this category. Assistants of all kinds, support staff of many descriptions, aides in a great variety of professions—all are servant positions in that their work contributes to projects or goals that are managed or directed by people to whom they are accountable. In an expanded sense, everyone who works for someone else in whatever capacity is, to that extent, a servant to the boss. In those situations where teamwork is truly integral to the work environment and where there is no immediate chain of command, the whole team is usually accountable to some other person or group. In that case, the team is a collective servant.

Working for someone else makes us essentially servants. Secretaries, then, are not the only people who think of themselves as servants. By extension and adaptation, the comments about secretaries are applicable to many workers. Most of us are servants to someone at work.

Being a servant is not bad. Some people interpret service as "bad" because of an exaggerated and erroneous belief in individualism. This version of individualism insists that people have a right to rule all aspects of their life, and that any accountability to anyone is an infringement on that basic right. This attitude is totally unsubstantiated and in fact contradicts both Christianity and the social aspect of human nature. While this viewpoint in its most drastic expression may not be too popular, there are vestiges of this brand of individualism that are more acceptable. The relationship between the individual and the community is complex, and the role of "servant versus master" is equally complicated. Some cultures stress the role of the community or group (Japan) while other cultures extol the values of the individual (U.S.A.). While there is no perfect arrangement between these two societal forces, it is valid to state that an extreme reliance on either pole of the individual-community continuum is an error. People who resent a service dimension in their work are most likely too close to the individualist pole of this relationship.

To repeat, being a servant is not bad. In fact, from a work-faith perspective, being a servant is an immediate and clear extension of the servant role of Jesus. Secretaries are servants to their bosses (whether they bring coffee or not!), even when the personal relationship is such that the boss and the secretary treat each other with mutual respect. The fundamental purpose of the secretarial position is to do things that make the boss' job easier or even possible. Secretaries can reflect on many passages of scripture and many faith themes that demonstrate the servant role of Jesus.

An obvious but powerful passage describes Jesus washing the feet of his disciples at the last supper (Jn 13). Even a cursory reading of this chapter leads to the clear conclusion that Jesus, the master, is also the servant. The message is unmistakable: Christians are fundamentally servants who are challenged to serve Jesus and to serve others, which in the final analysis is one and the same service.

The fact that the service performed by secretaries is part of their job assignment does not detract from the reality of the service. Willing service is more consistent with Jesus' example but even unwilling service remains service. Is the value of service dependent solely on the intention of the servant? No. While voluntary and wholehearted service is certainly closer to Jesus' role as servant/redeemer and therefore more meritorious, job-related service that is accomplished only because the job demands it is still service. Even disgruntled secretaries remain servants. Even inefficient secretaries are servants, though not very good ones. From the point of view of work-faith, the value of service is relative to the intention of and, to a lesser degree, to the capabilities of the secretary. But regardless of these variables, the job itself is still a service. And to the extent it is service, it imitates the role of Jesus/redeemer and therefore contributes to the kingdom.

Workfaith believers who are secretaries can make the connection between their work and their faith by reflecting on the service dimension of their job and the many references in scripture and church teaching to Jesus as servant. That connection is more than just semantics. Discovering this relationship can help secretaries, and all of us in similar roles integrate work with faith in a practical way that sheds light on our daily work activity.

Conclusion

The basic point of this chapter should now be clear: workfaith insists that all work activity, to some degree, contributes to God's kingdom. One way to specify the relationship between work and faith is to reflect on manufacturing jobs from the perspective of God as creator and to examine service jobs from the perspective of Jesus as redeemer/servant. Each of us who seeks to integrate faith and work more closely can search and discover how God is present in each workplace and each work effort. The reality of God's presence is simply an application of the fundamental belief that God is everywhere.

Workfaith does not limit the number of connections between faith and work. Most likely, there are a number of these connections in each job in each workplace. Multiple connections are not surprising: God's presence is personal and therefore complex. The more relationships between faith and work that believers can discover, the more enriching workfaith can be. When great numbers of us pray over, discuss and share our workfaith insights, the doors will open to a new level of faith experience. And if the Holy Spirit is at all predictable, this attention to faith and the workplace will inspire a new level of faith among millions of believers.

Study Questions

1. *Of the five manufacturing jobs outlined in this chapter, which one do you relate to most easily? Why? Does the workfaith analysis of this job make sense to you? Why, or why not?*

2. *Of the five service jobs outlined in this chapter, which one do you relate to most easily? Why? Does the workfaith analysis of this job make sense to you? Why, or why not?*

3. *Does the process of identifying God's presence on the job seem like a good way to nurture workfaith? Why?*

4. *Brainstorm about other ways in which Godpresence may be active in the ten jobs described in this chapter.*

5. *How could you deepen your sense of Godpresence in your specific job?*

4

Yes, But...

I don't like "Yes, buts ..." They confuse things when I want to clarify. I prefer the "say what you mean, and mean what you say" approach. A "yes, but ..." indicates that I haven't stated my position clearly enough the first time.

But with this chapter, I'm making an exception. I need a "yes, but ..." Workfaith opens the door to the mysterious presence of God at and in work. However, there is an immediate question: if all work is God's work, at least to some degree, then what about work that is evil? Work that intentionally harms others? Is God part of this evil work too? If so, how? If not, why not?

Those questions have to be addressed in any look at any workplace. All work environments have some "evil" along with the good, whether it's greed, pride or jealousy among workers, or producing a product that hurts people, or operating with procedures that are unethical, or a thousand other experiences and actions that are, to say the least, unloving. Evil is, and evil is in the workplace.

That's no big revelation. All of us who work can tell our own stories of our experience with some form of evil at work. The issue, then, is not whether there is evil at work. The issue is how can Godpresence co-exist with this evil, and what can we do to nurture the Godpresence and minimize the evil.

Obviously a detailed discussion of the mystery of good and evil would take us too far afield. But not dealing with it all would leave a big, obvious hole in this introduction to work-faith.

My goal here, then, is modest but significant. Hopefully, what can be shown is that the presence of evil does not exclude the presence of God. And since God is still present in the midst of the most horrifying evil, we can respond to that presence if we can wade through the evil and, in faith, find God.

Why does God permit evil? In the face of a Hitler, for example, why doesn't God just make him love others? Force the evil out of the madman! God could do it; God is all-powerful. Then why does God tolerate a Hitler—and all other people and events that cause unjust and obvious harm to innocent victims? And, on a lesser scale, why does God permit the evil we experience at work?

The final answer resides somewhere in the mysterious inner workings of the Trinity. If Jesus revealed the answer, as some Christians insist, then many of us just don't get it. Even believers can't explain it to the clear understanding of others. Faith maintains that there is an answer, and it's part of the passion, death and resurrection of Jesus. But even the most ardent believers admit that the mystery of evil continues. The mystery continues because the fact of evil is evident each and every day.

On the other hand, admitting the mystery does not mean all discussion is over. Helpful insights are still possible. For example, the presence of evil demonstrates the profound respect that God has for free will. God doesn't force the divine will on anyone. We are all free enough to be considered human. We are not totally free, but there are some choices we all make. Perhaps the most fundamental choice we have is the alternative between being selfish or loving. In some way or other, that choice is offered to all of us.

God simply does not tamper with our ability to choose. Even when the decisions are destructive, God does not interfere. That's how much God respects our freedom.

The dilemma is that if God did otherwise, our ability to choose would be destroyed, and, with it, humanity itself would end. If God forced us to love, it would not be love and we would no longer be people. On the operational level, the essence of love is that it is voluntary. To love means to choose to love. If there is no choice, there is no love.

God chooses to create people who are capable of loving, in the hope that we will freely choose to love God in return. The consequence of creating beings like us is that we can also choose evil in its many forms. It is the flip side of the ability to love. Without the ability to choose and do evil, we would also have to forego the ability to choose to love. God is so intent on offering the opportunity to love that this same God allows the evil choices we make.

It seems, then, that evil, including workplace evil, is generated by the evil choices we make. But are those choices the only source of evil? Many Christians also believe that evil emanates from evil spirits—the devil, Satan, personal beings outside human existence who have the ability to impact our lives. The scriptures speak frequently of these evil spirits who influence the health, actions and moral character of people and who seem to do what they want to whomever they choose at any time they decide—until they meet Jesus. The battle between Jesus and these evil spirits is a major theme of the gospels. In the end, of course, Jesus overcomes these devils. His death and resurrection delivers the final and unanswered blow to these powerful spirits that easily inflict evil of great magnitude and variety on us.

There are, then, two basic viewpoints, and many variations, on the source of evil: people are the source of evil and/or Satan is the source of evil. Which position is true? Most likely, the best answer accepts parts of each response and rejects extremes of each position. Those of us who claim that evil comes only from our evil choices neglect the existence and role of the spirit world. Those who insist on the exclusive role of Satan in causing evil neglect our capacity to choose evil and, ultimately, human freedom itself. How these two seemingly opposite realities are connected in a given situation is difficult, if not impossible, to determine. But any analysis which eliminates either viewpoint is fundamentally flawed.

The fact of evil is the result of both human activity and the influence of spirits.

The evil we experience at work is no different than the evil we experience anywhere else. But at work, it's harder to label these experiences as "evil" because we identify "good" and "evil" as religious labels which are inappropriate in a secular workplace. At work we deal with problems, policies and procedures, but not "evil."

Workfaith insists that we identify, nurture and celebrate Godpresence at work. The other side of the coin is that we also identify, contain and reject the evil at work.

The Christian Response to Evil

Before we become more specific about God and evil at work, we need to glance at the overall Christian response to evil. This glance will give us the context in which we can deal with evil on the job.

The heart of the Christian response to evil is, of course, Jesus. The gospels give continuous testimony that Jesus faces evil in the form of sickness, conspiracy, persecution, innocent suffering, his own passion and ultimately his execution. On a theological level, Jesus confronts the effects of sin and, though sinless himself, accepts the full consequences of sin, including death. Jesus does not run away from evil. His agony in the garden the night before his crucifixion is the most intense personal moment of his face to face confrontation with evil (Mk 14:32-42). This episode is the agony of decision making. Jesus is severely tempted; he begs his Father to "take this cup away from me." He truly wants to avoid this final conflict with evil and sincerely desires an alternative. But as we know, he resolves this temptation by accepting the will of the Father and proceeding with his passion and death.

Unquestionably, the Father could have taken a different approach. Instead, Jesus overcomes evil by accepting the effects of evil, and then by bringing good out of evil. The power of the resurrection could only happen after accepting the power of evil. God conquers evil by facing it head-on and going beyond death to a new kind of life.

It is this passage from death to new life that offers hope to us who also face evil in many forms. We share in the victory Jesus won against evil.

Evil is an abstract term. But we experience evil in very concrete terms. We use the term "evil" in many different ways, and what one person labels evil may not be considered evil by another person. For example, some people label a hurricane as evil. The devastation caused by the high winds and flooding may include death and millions of dollars in destruction. This calamity, to some people, is an evil caused by nature, Satan, or God. If God is named as the cause of the evil hurricane, then the "good" God created the evil hurricane to punish sinners or to test the faith of believers.

Other Christians look at the same hurricane and make no reference to the term "evil." For these people, evil is restricted to moral issues, those situations which are determined by choices between morally good or bad consequences. A hurricane, then, is not a moral good or evil; it is simply the convergence of certain atmospheric conditions which generate a natural reaction. These conditions are only indirectly related to God in that God, as creator of the universe, established the laws which periodically produce hurricanes. No "evil" is attached to these occurrences. These believers claim that there is no "fault" involved with hurricanes (or any event of nature). In fact, the existence of the hurricane is only a problem when it happens to move across an inhabited area. It isn't the hurricane's fault that people happen to live where it goes. And, in this view, it isn't God's fault either, since God doesn't direct the path of the hurricane. It isn't that God couldn't direct or dispel the hurricane; it simply means that God has chosen to allow natural law to take its course.

From this perspective, God could interfere with the laws of nature, and if God chooses to do so, the result would be a miracle. We believe that miracles happen but how often they happen and under what circumstances they happen is open to argument. The main point is that God has chosen not to interfere with natural law very often and that normal disasters are the result of nature, not God's personal intervention.

The word "evil" then has many different connotations. Some say that sickness is an evil; others say disease is an unfortunate but inevitable aspect of life. Some claim that accidents are evil; others maintain that accidents are just that—accidents.

I don't want to go any further in analyzing evil and the Christian response. The assumption here is that evil, specifically evil work, is limited to more obvious and generally accepted incidents of evil. Murder, illegal drug production and dealing, stealing, rape, large scale corruption, blatant discrimination, deliberate slaughter of innocent people—these are the kinds of activities most of us would agree are evil. The question of how God is present in these horrifying actions is the key to this chapter. If God can be identified even when these events take place, then God can be more easily discovered when events of less obvious evil take place. With this perspective, we will be able to identify, contain, and reduce the evil we experience on the job.

God and Work That Is Evil

Now let's take a more specific look at God and work that produces evil.

The victory of Jesus over sin and evil does not mean the struggle is over. It means that the eventual outcome has been guaranteed. Eternal life with the God who is love is available, despite all the pain, suffering and evil that still stalks the earth. Individual participation in this victory is not guaranteed, not without the required faith. The precise nature of this faith is disputed, but Jesus' triumph over sin and death is not an automatic ticket to skip the trials of life and immediately inherit the kingdom.

We know that the second coming of Jesus at the end of this world will be the occasion when all creation outwardly reflects the ultimate triumph of Jesus over evil. The essential battle has been won but the extension of the effects of this victory throughout the universe is still being accomplished.

In the meantime, evil continues both in the form of evil human choices and in the form of evil spirits somehow influencing human activity. Evil continues as long as there is a possibility that one person can still choose evil. And, as I mentioned earlier, since God chose to create us with the potential to love, the potential to sin and evil must remain.

Work that produces evil, therefore, is a large part of human experience. A work activity that produces evil must somehow co-exist with God's presence in and at the same work. How does this co-existence happen and what can we do about it?

The usual assumption is that in the presence of horrifying evil, God is not present and certainly not active. But such absence and such inactivity on God's part is impossible. God is always present and God is always active. An absent and inactive God is an absolute contradiction. By definition, God is both present and active—regardless of the overwhelming evil.

I want to describe this relationship between evil work and Godpresence through an example. The example outlines the evil, identifies the work component of this evil, and offers an explanation of how God is present and what we can do about it. If all work is God's work as described in chapter 3, then it is critical to discover the relationship between Godpresence and evil work.

Murder

The example is murder. It is intentionally gruesome, without mitigating circumstances. The idea is that if God can be discovered even in this obviously evil situation, then God can also be discovered along with the evil we experience in the workplace.

The particular circumstances of this murder include pre-meditation, a deliberate attack on a completely defenseless and innocent victim, and a murderer who remains remorse-less. The weapon is a gun, and the motive is a perceived but erroneous affront, i.e. the killer thought the victim made a comment the killer didn't like. The killer has a gun, takes a week to plan his attack, waits until the victim is alone, and shoots him five times in the back of the head. A neighbor hears the shots, calls the police immediately and a squad car just happens to be one block away at the time of the murder. The police arrive at the scene before the killer can escape and capture the murderer with the gun in his hand and absolutely no doubt that he killed the victim. He thought he could get away before the police would arrive, but he has no regrets about shooting the man. The killer has a history of violence—many fights, suspected of a previous murder but not enough evidence to arrest him, etc.

It is truly an open and shut case. There are no legal escapes and certainly no doubt that the killer committed the crime.

Where is God during this evil act?

Let's begin by asking a prior question: what is the work activity? Broken down into its component parts, the whole series of individual acts are work. The critical work action is pulling the trigger. Is God present in and during the actual evil work activity of pulling the trigger? Yes. Pulling the trigger is not evil in itself. The evil comes from deliberately pointing the gun at the victim and choosing to pull the trigger in order to commit murder. God is present through the whole process. In itself each specific work activity is a "good" action because the activity, separated from the circumstances, is a harmless action.

The main point is that the evil comes from the free and deliberate choice of the killer to commit murder. God doesn't choose to interfere with this human action. If God intervened, there would be no choice. And without the choice, there would be no free will. And without the free will, there would be no human being. And without the human being, there would be no chance for human love. And without love, there would be no chance for us to love God or each other.

God allows this terrible crime in order to protect the nature of the human being God created. And even during and within this work of murder, God is begging, pleading, calling for the murderer to recognize God's presence and love. God is screaming to be discovered. But God's pleading and screaming is not heard. The killer continues to choose evil and continues to ignore the presence of God and love.

When confronted with these kinds of episodes, we are disgusted by the event. Along with the outrage against the killer and the sympathy for the victim, there is also the painful awareness that God is present during the murder, witnessing the evil choice of one man killing another, both of whom are created in the image and likeness of God.

God surely wants to be discovered in these terrible crimes so the divine presence can be identified more clearly. That presence is evident in the many single acts that make up the whole series of actions which eventually lead to murder. The willful choice of the killer to commit murder is such a dominant factor in the whole process that the tendency is to consider only this choice in reacting to the crime. Without denying the centrality of this evil choice, it remains true that God is present in the individual acts. During each individual act God is hoping the killer will change his mind and choose to stop the killing process. Each separate step is an opportunity for the killer to reconsider. The fact that he proceeds with the evil plan doesn't negate the opportunity he had with each separate work activity to change his mind. Those continuing opportunities are the presence of God. These are the "good" that intermingle with the evil.

This example of murder is an exaggeration when compared with the "evil work" we face in our daily job experiences. But the process of discovering the presence of God within the murder is the same as discovering the presence of God within the evil at work. The murder case illustrates that God is actively present even in this horrible event. Along with predictable and justifiable anger, we can also discover God within the murder. The same thing is true with whatever workplace evil we identify.

So what? Recognizing the presence of God within the murder doesn't make the killer less guilty. In fact, the awareness that God is present may dramatize the horror of the crime. Why would we even *want* to think about God's presence in an event like that?

There really is only one answer: because it's true! The truth is a value in itself. Seeing this truth gives us one more glimpse at the mystery of God. The Father, Son and Holy Spirit are part of the murder scene, not causing it or condoning it. God is there trying to prevent it!

If God can't prevent it, then who can? Only the murderer with his/her ability to choose! Does this limit God, thereby making God not God? No! God chooses to respect our freedom and the consequences this freedom creates. In an absolute sense, certainly God has the power to interfere with our choices. But most often, God chooses to allow us to make our choices even when they cause evil.

When faced with these terrifying events, we can reflect on this part of the mystery of Godpresence. This reflection may lead to a variety of insights: the all-encompassing, never-ending presence of the Trinity, God's unimaginable respect for human freedom, the divine yearning for human love, the pain of sin that allows people to kill one another, and the power of the resurrection of Jesus which makes it possible to overcome even this evil.

It is this kind of faith that helps us discover Godpresence in and at work. But for this faith to be relevant and concrete, we must learn to practice this faith.

Faith Practice

We are often urged to practice our faith. It's a necessary reminder for most of us because it's easy enough to become complacent about living a truly Christian life each and every day. Even those of us who are deeply committed and fervent at one point in life can slip into a lukewarm observance of familiar religious practices. Mediocrity in prayer and compromise in moral matters lead to diminished faith, tarnished hope and faded love. Daily events can distract us from a focus on God and erode long held moral values.

The need to remind us of God's love and to accept the responsibilities that inevitably accompany Christian faith is evident. During those times of drifting faith it is helpful to hear the call to practice our faith. The call for renewal may come from preachers, writers, friends or family. Without it, we would likely fade into the secular culture and begin to take on some of the destructive values of the surrounding society.

In this setting we are urged to "practice" our faith. Normally this encouragement means that we are to "use" our faith which in turn means to *live* as we *say* we will live. Practicing faith implies that we are consistent in what we profess and in the way we act. We are not phony. We demonstrate by our behavior that our words are genuine. We practice in our life what we testify to by our words. "Practice what you preach" is the time honored slogan that summarizes the continual battle against hypocrisy and backsliding.

That's what "practice" usually means when applied to a faith context. I know that at different times in my life I have had to practice my faith in this sense. I have been distracted by job changes, stages in our kids' lives, or just plan routine daily living. I let my prayer life drift, my group life evaporate (I need some kind of small group going in order to keep me on my spiritual toes), and my spiritual reading remains on the shelf. Fortunately, after a while something or someone gets me back on track. I refocus. I "practice" my faith more honestly.

There is, however, another equally legitimate use of the

term "practice." This meaning reflects that part of the definition which stresses the need to repeat a procedure in order to
become more skilled or proficient at a given activity. A basketball player practices shooting baskets in order to score more
points more proficiently. A ballerina practices a dance in
order to perform flawlessly. A typist practices keystrokes in
order to increase speed and accuracy while typing. It goes on
and on—we practice in order to become more skilled or to
upgrade an unfamiliar activity into an accustomed habit.

The notion of "practice" also has a long tradition within
Christianity. Various forms of spirituality insist that followers
practice virtues and disciplines in order to drive away sinful
tendencies or to develop specific character traits. Many devo-
tions, prayers and actions (fasting, almsgiving, self-induced
suffering, etc.) are some examples. In many cases, these repetitious activities seem to work, i.e. practitioners appear to
become holier people while performing these actions. Of
course, practice alone doesn't automatically make us holy.
Faith remains as a necessary component of Christian holiness.

But faith too can be practiced in the sense that repetitious
acts can increase faith. Undoubtedly, faith is always a gift of
God. The initial experience of faith is freely granted by God,
and it is a gift that is not merited or earned. In some way or
another, this gift is offered to all of us. No one knows how
God accomplishes this offering, nor how each of us responds.
Some of us seem to respond positively while others seem to
reject the gift and refuse to believe. In the final analysis, however, the judgment about who accepts the gift of faith and
who denies it must be left to God and each of us.

The story doesn't end with the acceptance of initial faith.
Faith is not a gift to be put on the shelf and pulled out when
convenient. The gift is not a "thing" at all. The gift is a relationship with God. Faith is our response to God's love. Since
faith is fundamentally the recognition and acceptance that
there is a loving God, this faith can grow or wane. There can

be intense recognition and acceptance, or there can be minimal recognition and slight acceptance.

Practicing the gift of faith, then, is an exercise that can increase the recognition and acceptance of the presence of God. This aspect of faith is very much like the practice by the basketball player, the ballerina, or the typist. Many of the same principles apply: conscious repetitious acts until they become routine; times dedicated to practice; overcoming boredom; conviction that the practice is worth it; following a reliable pattern (practice doesn't make perfect—perfect practice makes perfect); accept limitations and don't be discouraged by comparisons with others.

All of these principles apply to faith practice. The obvious difference is that faith deals with a relationship with God while other practice activities deal with improving skills or a desire to compete. Regardless of these differences, there are similarities that are worth pursuing.

Specifically, faith practice means to consciously view experiences and events by adding the dimension of Godpresence. How is God present and what is God doing during this experience or event? Faith practice attempts to answer these questions as explicitly as possible. Admittedly, these answers are speculative, and some of us may answer them somewhat differently than others. Guidance for the answers must come from scripture and the teachings of the church. But this guidance is often generic, i.e. if the interpretation of how God is present and what God is doing in any given event does not violate scripture or church dogmas, that interpretation may be valid for specific believers. Revelation is the guide, but God can communicate to individuals and communities in whatever way God chooses to communicate.

The speculative answers about how God is present and what God is doing can be extremely valuable in nurturing the gift of faith. It is simply to say that since God is present all the time, it is helpful to learn how to discover that presence. Faith practice increases the skill of finding God in our daily life.

How To Practice

I need directions. When I have to assemble something—bookcases, toys, small appliances, anything that remotely deals with electricity—I need lots of directions. When I started jogging, I needed specific instructions on what muscles to stretch and how to stretch them prior to my little run and what to do after I came panting home. When I cook, the recipe had better be clear—none of this "a little dash of this and a little bit of that". When I get a work assignment that isn't obvious, I ask a lot of questions.

The same attitude applies to faith. When I say "practice my faith," I want a step-by-step process on how to practice my faith. General goals are nice and somewhat helpful, but I need directions on how to reach the goal. I am not alone in this need.

The following process is an outline, and you can certainly adjust it to meet your approach and needs. It includes the major steps in practicing faith in the sense that we can learn to see the world and ourselves more consistently through the eyes of faith. It literally takes practice. The desire to increase our faith is commendable, but without directions on how to do it, we can lose our desire very quickly.

Step 1: Choose a recent event.

This event may be a recent news item or a personal experience. It is important to identify a current event in order to avoid reflecting too much on the past. At this point, the concentration is on God's presence in today's events so that we can practice finding God in current events and experiences.

Some events more obviously lend themselves to discovering the presence of God than others. For example, a news story about Mother Teresa ministering to the poor of Calcutta will easily lead us to discover Jesus and God in that ministry. A story, however, about a serial killer or devastating hunger in Africa or job lay-offs will probably be more difficult to pinpoint. For the sake of faith practice, then, the first choices should be some experiences that are not too challenging. Like any other practice project, start with the easy and progress to the more difficult.

At the beginning, it is also better to start with "objective" events like a news story, a book or a magazine article. Often personal experiences are complicated by personal motives, subconscious forces, or inappropriate emotions. After three or four faith practice exercises with more objective events, and an acceptable comfort level is achieved with the process, then proceed to the more complicated personal experiences and the more challenging objective events.

Choose a specific event rather than a general theme like "the economy." God is present to the economy in many specific ways: economic policy making, worker lay-offs, individuals filing for bankruptcy, tax cuts, pay raises, etc. The event needs to be specific so that the specific presence of God can be discovered more clearly.

Step 2: Reflection: God is present in and through this event.

This reflection is necessary because we are not aware of the presence of God within these events. The purpose of this step is not to enable us to be conscious of Godpresence all the time. This constant awareness is not bad, of course, but most of us are simply not capable of continual awareness. We must focus on other issues—the person we are dealing with, the project at hand, the problem to be solved, the moment to be enjoyed, etc. The goal here is not total and exclusive concentration on Godpresence at all times. The goal in Step 2 is an improved recognition and acceptance of Godpresence in all events and particularly in workplace events.

There is no specific time frame for this reflection. It should be more than a cursory thought but not so long that it makes the process cumbersome. The focus of this step is the belief that, regardless of how evil the event is, God is still present in and through the event. Step 2 does not ask the question of how God is present. This stage is reflection on a faith statement: God *is* present. Period. That reality must be appreciated. Wonder, praise, gratitude, and acceptance are all appropriate reactions to this reflection.

Step 3: Question: What is God doing here?

Now is the time to ask the question of what God is doing here. Scripture, church teaching, inspirational reading, discussions with other people, personal thinking, and, of course, prayer are all tools to help answer this question. Draw upon all the resources available. Some of the comments in this chapter and in the previous chapter of this book are examples of the kind of thinking that could be helpful in answering this question.

There is a simple answer that applies to all situations. What God is always doing is loving. That's always the inevitable answer. That's what God does for a living! Love is the necessary starting point for any fuller response. The challenge is to discover more explicitly how God's love is active in a given situation. That's when the available resources can help shed light.

Even in the most destructive situations, like the murder described earlier, God is a loving presence. If we are seeking a fuller, more integrated faith life we will attempt to recognize and accept that loving presence more often and more clearly. Step 3 invites us to continue that search.

Step 4: Question: What do we do as a result of 1,2 and 3?

This faith practice process can lead us to deeper faith, increased hope and greater love. What we must do is "open" ourselves. To be "open" implies the removal of personal obstacles to faith, hope and love. These stumbling blocks can be anything from pride to negativism to fear to a wide variety of hidden insecurities and many other faults and character defects.

Identifying and removing these personal obstacles is the most significant action we can take if we wish to open ourselves to the loving presence of God. This removal is usually not easy. Long term habits of negative thinking and acting are so deeply rooted that they resist accurate identification and fight against removal.

There are many prescriptions for dealing with these obstacles to faith growth. Every form of spirituality has an approach and an emphasis. Each of us needs to find a way to face our sins and character defects. Without this fundamental confrontation with personal evil, we will not be able to discover the loving presence of God in any meaningful way. We are sinners, as well as saints, and we suffer from the effects of both personal and communal sin.

One positive method for dealing with these obstacles is to practice the virtues of prudence, justice, fortitude and temperance. These are the cardinal virtues, that is, they are hinges on which many other virtues revolve. Spend a month on each of these four virtues. Learn what each one means, examine yourself honestly on how well you live each virtue, identify strengths and weaknesses related to each virtue, make a plan for being more prudent, just, courageous and moderate. Pray for growth in each of these areas.

When we are more prudent, just, courageous and temperate, we are more likely able to remove the obstacles to faith, hope and love.

When these stumbling blocks are removed or minimized, we will recognize and accept the love of God even in those events that are overwhelmingly evil.

This four step process gives us an organized approach to practicing our faith. This practice may not literally make us perfect, but without this practice, improvement in recognizing and accepting the presence of God is unlikely. And without this improvement, an integrated faith life is wishful thinking.

This process is neither "fundamentalist" nor "progressive." It is beyond ideological labels. It is a method to identify the presence of God. The presence of God is basic to all forms of Christianity—the conservative wing of Catholicism, mainline

Protestantism, fundamentalism, pentecostalism and evange-
lism. All Christians, by definition, believe in the loving presence of God. Discovering, nurturing and celebrating that
presence is essential to any authentic Christian.

Faith Practice and Work

This faith practice technique is useful for all aspects of life.
It is, however, definitely needed when the focus switches to
the workplace. The workplace officially ignores the presence
of God and, in fact, promotes the inadvertent denial of
Godpresence. Because of this programmed secular view of the
workplace, it takes even more practice to discover God at
work than in many other parts of society.

If we can recognize and accept the presence of God even in
overwhelmingly evil activities like murder, then the possibility
of discovering the loving presence of God in the workplace
becomes more attainable. Practicing faith is one way to open
our eyes so we can discover this Godpresence at work—and
everywhere!

Study Questions

*1. In your own words, describe how God is present even
when "evil" is present.*

*2. Identify the most negative ("evil") aspect of your job. How
is God present even when this negative reality is active?
How does a workfaith believer deal with these situations?*

*3. How could the negative aspects (evil) of your job strength-
en your spirituality?*

*4. Exercise: Each person follows the process outlined in this
chapter about applying workfaith to his/her job (pgs. 92-
94). One person at a time shares his/her answers to the
questions in the process. Personalize your responses as
much as possible. After everyone has shared their responses, discuss similarities and differences in the responses.*

5

Forces at Work

Walk into any workplace—factory, office, store, shop, department, some combination of the above or something totally different—and you'll notice that there's something in the air. It has different names: the work culture, environment, emotional climate, or atmosphere, to name a few. It's hard to pin down and label, but it's very real. Almost all of us can sense it, even when we can't name it.

Whatever it's called, everyone has to adjust to it. Some people accept it without too much difficulty, while others fight against it and attempt to change it. Some workers identify it very clearly while others attempt to ignore it. Some of it comes from the local combination of people, the goals of the organization, the nature of the business and the traditions of the company. Some of it comes from the more general business climate, the state of the economy and worldwide trends. Some of it seems to be controllable by local people while some of it seems completely beyond anyone's control. In any case, it exists and it's powerful. It must be considered in any adequate look at any workplace.

For our purposes here, "it" is called "forces at work." The choice of the term "forces" is deliberate because it seems to represent the reality more accurately than the other alternatives. A "force" implies a power or an energy that affects someone or something. A force attempts to move people or things in a specific direction, and that movement is precisely what we feel at work.

These forces help determine the nature of the overall work experience. They change from century to century, culture to culture, country to country and company to company. These forces reflect the values of the current society and usually rein-force these values. In a broad perspective, these movements at work mirror the general economic and social philosophy of the society. In its most generic terms the economy is either free or controlled. A capitalist society leans toward free enterprise while a socialist, communist or dictatorial society leans toward structure and/or government control. Many economies today combine features from pure capitalism and pure socialism. Theoretically the combination is supposed to minimize the dif-ficulties with both approaches, i.e. the strengths of capitalism keep the weaknesses of socialism in check, while the advan-tages of socialism restrain the excesses of capitalism.

How successful these varied economies are is not the point. The observation here is that regardless of the content of the prevailing economic philosophy, it has a definite impact on the work experience of every worker in every job. For example, because of these forces an automobile worker in the U.S.A. will have a different work experience than a similar worker in Japan. It may also be that an auto worker at G.M. may have a significantly different work life than an auto worker at Ford. The "forces" in each company may be so dif-ferent that the work experiences have little in common other than that they ultimately produce cars.

Many of these forces are contrasting. One force may stress one value and another force may emphasize an opposing value. These contrasting values can create tension and incon-sistency. It's often not a matter of good versus evil, but the acceptance of the fact that life is a combination of many movements experienced simultaneously. Emphasis on one force at a given time is acceptable. But each force has its counter-force and over a long period of time the emphasis in one direction will lead to problems because the opposing force also has value. Eventually this contrary force must be incorporated in order to offset the weakness of the currently prominent force. We refer to this constant swing between opposing forces as the "pendulum effect."

We have to reflect on these forces because they have a major impact on our work life. Not every workplace has all of these forces and certainly not in the same configuration. Each workplace has its own culture in the sense that the combination of forces that are "in the air" is unique to each place and probably to each job. The intent here is to identify seven major forces which seem to influence many jobs. How these forces affect your job will be your task. The purpose here is to describe these seven forces and then suggest ways in which we might begin to respond to these forces from a workfaith perspective. The intention, then, is to "prime the pump" in the hope that further reflection and discussion will generate more precise understanding and acceptance of the presence of God in the workplace.

The seven forces at work are: competition, women in the workplace, management versus labor, regulations, marketing, globalization and technology. There are undoubtedly other trends or forces that are operative in your workplace but these seven seem to be very extensive, and they warrant a closer look. If you identify other major forces, I suggest you adopt an approach similar to the one used here.

Competition

In an economy that allows free enterprise even in limited forms, competition is essential. The basic theory is that competition develops improved products and motivates workers to produce a product or service with ever increasing standards of quality and productivity. Competition spurs people on and measures the success of the company or department. The proponents of this theory also maintain that, without competition, the measuring stick for quality, productivity and success is arbitrary.

Obviously, some jobs are more competitive than others. Selling cars was the most competitive job I had, but the airline industry is also very competitive. Teaching and educational administration is not as immediately and inherently competitive. But even in these positions there is competition in that students vie with each other over grades, and teachers and schools often make comparisons with each other. Pastoral ministry in general is competitive because we try to entice people to participate with their time, talent and money when these same people could spend their time, talent and money on other things. In varying degrees, then, I have experienced competition in all of my jobs. Most of you can easily identify the competitive dimension to your job.

In and of itself, competition is neither good nor evil. Competition can motivate us. It can also lead us to greed, destructive power, and disregard for the rights of others. Which direction competition takes depends on the competitor.

Some of you are very competitive and you lead loving, stable, productive and fulfilling lives. Some of you can care less about "winning or losing," and lead loving, stable, productive and fulfilling lives. Some of you combine competitiveness and non-competitiveness and lead loving, stable, productive and fulfilling lives. On the personal level, there is no "better or worse" when it comes to competition. It all depends on how we handle our personalities.

On the work level, competition is inevitable. Whether we work in the public or private sectors, there is some level of competition "in the air." Those of us who are personally competitive and work in an obviously competitive position will probably rise or fall depending on whether we win or lose. Those of us who are neither personally competitive nor experience competition too obviously in the workplace will not be as affected by the whims of competition.

In private industry, competition is evident in that products and services either sell or they don't. Sufficient revenue is either generated or it isn't, and the results are either profit or loss. If the company is profitable, the work environment is free of the tension associated with failing companies. If the company is losing money, the insecurity for all the employees becomes an everyday cause of anxiety.

Employees in the government sector, either military, education, health care or any other agency, deal with competition in the sense that they all need tax dollars to support their programs. The constant tug between raising and spending tax money is a form of competition that infiltrates the worklife of all government employees.

How do we deal with competition from a workfaith perspective? The basic principle is that competition reinforces the desire to produce an ever-improving product or service. The emphasis is always on developing a better product/service, not on beating a competitor for the sake of winning or power or even to make more money than the other guy.

The focus is on self-motivation, on looking at our company or department with the conviction that dedication to doing the best that current resources allow will translate into a competitive edge against other companies that produce a similar product or service. The strategy is to constantly seek new and better ways to design, develop, manufacture and market the company's product/service. New technology, shifting trends, improved delivery methods, breakthrough approaches, new worldwide or local economic factors—they all provide many opportunities for companies or departments to improve their product/service in order to guarantee continued success.

If a rival company comes up with an improved product/service, or a manufacturing technique that saves money, or a marketing tactic that works, then we can seek ways to adapt the innovation in a way that is appropriate to our company. The key is to use this competitive disadvantage in order to improve our product, not out of anger at the competitor but out of a fierce desire to do or produce the best we can.

We must approach the reality of competition with some caution. Christian principles insist that competitors must be treated fairly, with respect and even love. There is no room for motivation to produce or succeed based on hating the other guys or tearing down a competitor's product or undermining their approach. There is room only for the healthy competition that centers on personal improvement, measured against either personal goals or industry-wide achievements. Competitive anger must be self-anger, directed internally at why our product/service isn't better.

Does this approach imply that we become easy prey to unscrupulous rivals? Not at all! It simply means that competition is tough but self-directed rather than blaming and attacking other people or companies. Whether the competition is between companies or within the workplace (for promotions, job assignments, office space, etc.) we are not "pushovers" because we are workfaith believers. We present our opinions as strongly as we can. What we will not do, however, is undermine a competitor. We will emphasize the advantages of our position without degrading or misrepresenting the advantages of the competing product or service.

Maintaining this perspective in some work environments will not be easy. If the overwhelming force is negative competition, we will be at odds with our prevailing work culture. We may be required to compromise in the sense that we really have no choice about a particular policy, procedure or decision. Compromise, of course, is not desired but it is acceptable—up to a point! There may be work situations which are so negative, so competitive that we have to seek another job. Where the line is between acceptable work competition and an unacceptable situation will have to be decided by each of us.

The point here is that the competitive environment does not have to be completely "pure" in order for us to function effectively. On the other hand, it is possible that the competitive atmosphere is so destructive that leaving is the only alternative. Most situations are somewhere in between these two

extremes. Most situations, then, are at least minimally acceptable from a workfaith perspective.

In any case, regardless of how destructive the competition
is, God is still present, urging the competitors to love one
another even as they compete fiercely with each other. Is this
combination of love and competition possible? Yes! But it
takes attention, courage, prayer and commitment.

The greatest hurdle to living this possibility is the belief
that it isn't possible. Far too often, the assumption is that the
workplace is so competitive that God and genuine believers
can't live with it. That's nonsense! When we give ourselves
"permission" to think in terms of combining competition and
love, we are able to do it. The specifics of how this happens
in each person's worklife depends on many factors but it's
not as hard as many of us assume. The first step is to try it.

Love and competition are not opposites. The opposite of
love is fear. Eliminate the mind set that the business world is so
competitive that love cannot co-exist and many of the obstacles
will vanish. There is no need to fear competition in the workplace. Erase the fear and seek the love! The amazing result will
be to discover not only love but also healthy competition.

Women in the Workplace

Women, of course, have always worked. In recent decades,
however, there has been an increasing effort to demonstrate
that most jobs are gender neutral. That effort, and the
changes that accompany it, present a workplace today that
frees women, and men, from stereotypical roles. The changing role of women in the workplace is an unquestioned fact
of the current workplace.

I have always been in jobs where women were co-workers.
In fact, for five years when I was a parish director of religious
education, my wife and I had the same basic job description,
shared an office, reported to the same pastor/boss and co-
sponsored many adult education programs. Friends of ours
claim that they could never work with their spouse. Our

experience was very positive, both in terms of our professional performance and our personal relationship.

In other positions, I have worked with and worked for a
variety of women. That fact is no longer astounding. Women
in all kinds of work roles are rapidly becoming natural,
expected, and taken for granted. Gender neutrality is becoming the norm. Sexual discrimination is still a disturbing factor
in many places and the specifics of gender neutrality are not
all clear but at this point the momentum continues to build
for more roles and equal treatment for women.

This glance at women in the workplace is not a debate,
prediction or appeal. It is simply a statement that the workplace is moving in the direction of gender neutrality and it
indicates a workfaith response to this trend.

The number of women in the workplace increases daily
and the kind of positions they hold also is expanding rapidly.
In many ways, the workplace reflects society. The changing
role of women in society has its counterpart in the workplace, but since the workplace is a regulated environment,
discrimination is patrolled. Equality is the stated goal. But this
equality is voluntary throughout much of society. At work it is
required. Some of you, both men and women, do not approve
of these changes in the roles of women. You prefer things the
way they used to be.

Increasingly, this type of gender stereotyping will get you
in trouble. The law, and company policy, follows the direction of the courts. Policies are responsive to legal cases: one
man/woman objects to behavior that reflects some degree of
sexual discrimination or prejudice, files a complaint or a suit,
wins the case and the company must adopt the ruling, even if
90% of the people don't find the behavior personally offen-
sive. In this area, as in other areas of discrimination or safety,
we are not a country of popular opinion or majority rule. We
are a country of protected rights and law. Therefore, if one
person wins a case, company policy must follow the directives of that case.

In this sense, the workplace not only reflects the values of society, the workplace leads society in implementing gender neutrality. It has no choice. Worker attitudes may not agree with these gender policies but workplace managers and owners must follow the gender neutral policies of the courts.

In practice, then, we probably experience gender neutrality on the job more so than any other place in society. You may get away with an inappropriate joke or comment in the neighborhood or your own home, but that same joke or comment could get you in a lot of trouble at work. While this kind of behavioral control does not guarantee attitudinal change, it does provide an arena where gender neutrality is at least superficially respected.

Workfaith calls for love and respect between the genders. Prejudice and discrimination in any form is rejected. We must think and act beyond stereotypes. Women are not sex objects and limited to support staff functions. Men are not the exclusive decision makers. Both men and women receive equal opportunities to demonstrate their ability to perform according to the same set of standards in all functions. There are no "men jobs" and "women jobs"; there are only jobs that require certain skills, and whoever can perform those skills at an acceptable level deserves an equal chance, and equal pay, for that position. Workfaith implies this equality.

This equality does not deny nor neglect the reality of gender appeal. Very often, the workplace is where men and women become close professionally and personally. Friendships are formed; some of these friendships are same-sex relationships and some are opposite-sex friendships. In the workplace, people, regardless of gender, must work together. The regulated environment provides an opportunity for us to go beyond and through gender issues in order to work side by side for a common goal. The fact that sometimes these relationships go too far or become unhealthy or unloving does not negate the opportunity the workplace provides.

The tension between the sexes has long been a part of the

human experience. The workplace, with its recent emphasis on gender neutrality, will not eliminate this tension. But the workplace, perhaps reluctantly, is gradually becoming a leader in setting up opportunities for sexual respect and genuine, healthy love between men and women.

Management Versus Labor

Every workplace has managers and workers, not that managers don't work or workers can't manage. In every company or department there are those people who primarily plan, organize, evaluate, motivate and make final decisions. There are also those who carry out the plans, implement the procedures, and perform all the tasks that are necessary to make the plans successful. This division of function is the classic view of modern management.

In recent years the classic model is becoming blurred in many companies. Traditional management functions like planning, organizing, evaluating and decision making are being shared with the entire workforce. The theory is that all employees have a stake in the company and the company will perform better if all the people act like owners and take responsibility for new ideas and better ways of doing things. Decision making becomes a shared task as managers seek consensus on more and more aspects of the workplace. Group problem solving replaces the traditional practice of the boss trying to solve all the problems and the workers trying to make these solutions fit the actual problems.

Even in those situations where decision making and problem solving is spread throughout the workforce, there remains the distinction between management and labor. In some settings this relationship is clearly defined and specific aspects of the work environment is formalized in a contract. In its clearest expression these relationships are represented in union contracts. The union exists in order to negotiate, represent and defend the rights, safety and welfare of the workers. The belief is that the workers, joined together in a common bond, will have a better chance of receiving beneficial treatment than individual workers negotiating alone with management.

There is no need here to review the history of the union movement, its pros and cons, its place in the modern workplace or its future. The focus here is to mention the union as one expression of the universal reality of the division of functions in any workplace. There is always some management, someone who is ultimately responsible for making sure that the final product or service is in fact delivered to the customer. There are always some other workers who will carry out the procedures needed to deliver that product or service.

Perhaps the tension between management and labor is inevitable. For the most part this relationship may be very cordial, with mutually agreed goals and procedures. But it often happens that conflicts arise. There may be a pending lay off, a change in workplace rules, an attempt at greater efficiency, the introduction of new technology or a hundred other issues that have many legitimate perspectives. At these times, management is generally interested in greater productivity while labor, represented by a union or not, is interested primarily in protecting jobs or advancing the benefits of the workers. Both of these goals are good in themselves, but working them out in concrete situations is often difficult. Management can misuse or abuse workers in the name of productivity. Labor can bankrupt the company in insisting on certain benefits for workers. In between these extremes, management and labor attempt to arrive at arrangements that are at least acceptable to all parties.

What is the proper attitude for workfaith believers, whether we are management or labor? Whose side are we on? We are on both sides because both sides represent values that are consistent with the gospel and the kingdom. The nature of the issues and the circumstances of the case may lead to confrontation. Neither management nor labor may want to make any more concessions, and an impasse may result. The threat of a strike or a lockout may harden the positions further. What do we do in these cases?

Throughout all of these deliberations and, indeed, through-out the entire work experience, we must maintain some basic principles. Whether management or labor, we will always treat the other side with respect. We will never allow personal issues to interfere with resolving the problems, e.g. to use this negotiation or issue primarily as an opportunity to promote a personal career. We will argue out of conviction that our posi-tion is correct and that our solution is the best answer for everyone. We will not proceed out of a motive of ego, or of the sheer desire to compete, argue or confront. We will not resort to name calling, lying or double talk. We will continue to seek solutions, even during an impasse.

Because we maintain an obvious respect for our opponents, even though we strongly disagree with them, we might be accused of being "too nice" or not strong enough to speak for either management or labor. Not true! We can also be very strong, persistent and, after a certain point, uncompromising. We can stick to our position and be convinced that our posi-tion is in fact the best way to proceed.

In essence, we workfaith believers attempt to improve the loving community at work while we keep an eye on profit. We may be union presidents or company presidents, and we may oppose each other across the negotiating table. And yet, we may both be genuine believers. But if a union president is intending to destroy the company, or the company president is attempting to destroy the union, they are going beyond what is consistent with workfaith.

Cynics say that management and labor will never get along. Their interests are mutually exclusive and they are fundamen-tally adversaries. While they may be cordial in certain settings, they never forget their inescapable opposition.

We take a different stance. We admit to differing positions on some critical issues, and yet we maintain a basic respect for the opponents. We resist the common temptation to judge the motives, values and character of the other side. For many of us, it is easier to fight when we judge the other side to be dumb, vile, evil, irresponsible, selfish or a thousand other damning adjectives. This perspective is not easy, and living it consistently is a major accomplishment; it is not minimal or trivial. It is workfaith in practice, and it is critical for those of us who wish to resolve the tension between management and labor, and who want to integrate work and faith.

Regulations

Regardless of the workplace, at some level there are government regulations. Whether it's regulations to protect the employee, the consumer, the environment, the market or the common good, government regulations are an integral part of every workplace.

There is an on-going debate regarding the nature and extent of these regulations. One side maintains that the less the government is involved, the better everyone will be. The other side claims that the government must be deeply involved in order to prevent exploitation. Once again, workfaith believers are found on both sides.

Few of us would argue that the government has absolutely no role in the marketplace. The purpose of government is to protect the common good, and many workplaces have an immediate impact on the common good. For example, a factory that produces toxic fumes must be held accountable and prevented from releasing those fumes. Most of us agree that the government (city, state or federal) is the appropriate agency to prohibit the factory from releasing lethal gas.

For two summers while I was in school I worked at a foundry that produced zinc. I was a laborer and it was hot, dirty work that included rotating shifts from days, afternoons and midnights each week. I liked the contrast with the study that occupied most of my time in those years. The foundry eventually closed but I found out much later that the acid fumes I was exposed to during those summers caused some permanent damage to my eyes. I was attempting to adjust my contact lens when my optometrist asked me if I was ever exposed to fumes. He explained that I had "callouses" over my eyes which were probably caused by an irritant in the air. When I mentioned my summers at the zinc foundry, he quickly concluded that those acid fumes caused my eye problem. Among other things I couldn't adjust my lenses and I now wear glasses.

Frankly, it's no big deal. I am content with wearing glasses (tri-focals, at this point!). But I prefer to wear contacts. If there would have been a law at the time regulating those fumes, perhaps I could be wearing contacts today. It's a minor issue, but it is my story. There are many other people with many more serious stories that demonstrate the need for some regulation in the workplace.

The fundamental role of the government is not the issue. The argument revolves around the extent of the regulations. How many regulations? How specific do they need to be? What areas really need regulating? What are the consequences for violating a regulatory law? Those are some of the debatable questions, but the basic right and duty of the government to protect the common good with some regulation of the workplace is generally accepted.

Workfaith believers argue these questions along with other people. But we also have a faith perspective which provides a context and some limits to the discussions.

For example, government regulations are a reminder that no place is totally sovereign. Every place, including work, is ultimately dependent on God. In dealing with regulations, then, we can accept these rules and laws as examples of an outside agency with some authority over the work environment. Of course, the government is not a substitute god or even representing God's will. In some cases, these regulations reflect God's will and in some cases they may not. And in many cases even ardent workfaith believers may not be able to determine if a particular regulation represents God's will or not.

The overall context, however, reminds us that no work situation is completely independent of God. In the final analysis, if a specific work rule or procedure contradicts the law of God, we must choose God's law over the work rules even if it means losing a job. There are many gray areas when a particular work project or activity runs somewhat against God's will. Fortunately, however, there are few jobs that demand activity that is clearly and seriously contrary to God's law. If that situation does arise, we must seek counsel, determine what the options are, and, if necessary, find work elsewhere. In our society, the need to make that decision is rare.

From another perspective, government regulations are a symbol of the larger loving community that the work community participates in. If the work group is basically a loving community as described earlier, then the whole world is also fundamentally a loving community, although at times it may be light years away from functioning as a worldwide loving community. The world may be a very poor example of a loving community, but essentially that's what it is.

Regulations represent that wider community. They insist that each workplace has a responsibility to this wider community. This connection to the "outside world" has nothing to do with the direct mission of the company or potential clients for the service organization. Government regulations remind each workplace that there is more to work than achieving the goals of the company. Even at work, we cannot ignore the demands of the wider community. That is as it should be.

Regulations by agencies outside the company may be a cause of irritation to some of us. And in some cases, this irritation may be completely justified. But workfaith believers, even as we criticize specific regulations, will accept the basic role of regulations as a legitimate representation of the world community and the need to be concerned about the kingdom of God in its worldwide dimensions.

Marketing

In one way or another all work is related to a market. Simply put, everything that is made or every service that is

offered must ultimately be used by someone. Marketing refers
to the process which attempts to convince a potential user to
buy a particular product or service. In effect, marketing
informs people about the nature and benefits of a product or
service in the hope that a sufficient number of people will
pay an adequate price for that product or service.

Included in marketing is advertising, selling, the reputation
of the company or product, public relations, research and
competitive analysis. It's a complicated part of the work
process, and often its success will determine the future worklife of all the employees.

Even workers with so-called guaranteed lifetime jobs are
not immune to the marketplace. First of all, if the company or
government agency runs out of money and if even Chapter 11
bankruptcy reorganization doesn't solve the problems, the
presumed lifetime guarantee is over. Secondly, downsizing
companies will cut certain jobs when executives consider it
necessary. Period. Government agencies are no absolute security either; they can easily be reorganized with subsequent
loss of employment to large numbers of people. Thirdly, job
assignments can be changed in such a way that individual
employees wind up doing distasteful and lower paying tasks,
which may not force them into unemployment but which can
make their work situation very unsatisfying.

Without successful marketing, all employees can suffer.
Even workers who have no respect for the marketing function, who think they are not related to marketing, are in fact
dependent on the use of their product or service by someone
else. Therefore, they too must rely on the market.

As a result, marketing is a prevailing force at work for
everyone.

A basic marketing strategy is to highlight the advantages of
the product and to ignore or minimize its disadvantages. That
strategy seems obvious. But it can be more complex than it
appears at first. For example, the low cost of a product
appears to be an advantage. And it usually is. But within a cer-

tain group of wealthy consumers, low cost may appear to be low quality and they will not buy the product. In these markets, a higher price may actually increase sales. In this case, a more expensive price tag becomes an advantage rather than a disadvantage.

Marketing, then, means to know the actual and perceived benefits of the product or service and to present these benefits in convincing ways to potential customers.

How do we workfaith believers, regardless of our job, deal with the marketing force at work? The issue here is truth and honesty. The people directly responsible for the marketing function may at times be tempted to so emphasize the benefits of their product that they misrepresent these benefits. They may not actually lie, and there are "truth in advertising" laws which are intended to protect consumers from false advertising. But there is a relatively large spectrum between the absolute, complete truth and a deliberate lie. Generally, the marketing people will draw attention to key benefits and ignore any possible liabilities. While this approach is not lying, in desperate situations the temptation is to cover up disadvantages by denying the liabilities and lying slips into the marketing plan.

Even though all workers will have to contend with marketing in some way, those workfaith believers who are in sales, public relations or advertising will have greater responsibility for marketing than other workers. To remain consistent with their faith, marketing believers will have to promote the benefits of their product but not lie about its liabilities. If asked, they will have to admit the negative aspects of their product and attempt to convince the customer that the benefits outweigh the disadvantages, and hope enough customers buy the product. These workfaith believers must never lie or deliberately mislead customers. To do so would so compromise their faith that integrating work with faith may be impossible.

Can these workfaith believers be truly honest and still sell their products? Yes! Many already do! These are people who have an active and informed conscience and who know the lines between presenting the benefits of a product and misleading a consumer. They know these lines because along with learning the techniques of marketing, selling or public relations, they also developed their conscience in these areas. They prayed, studied, read and sought counsel precisely in this area of honesty. They know the moral principles involved and they know how far they can go. As they became specialists in marketing, they also became specialists in workfaith as it applies to marketing. Their reward for this extra effort is the knowledge that they can in fact integrate their work with their faith. They are comfortable with themselves both as believers and as workers. As a result, they are better prepared to discover and respond to Godpresence within their work.

It is beneficial for all of us to reflect on the marketing aspect of our work. Not everyone will have to be as knowledgeable and proficient at these aspects of marketing and honesty as those employees who are directly involved with these functions. But since all employees are affected by and participate in the marketing aspect of the company in some way, it is necessary for all of us to respond to this force at work. Perhaps the most practical way to respond effectively is for those of us who are not marketing specialists to discuss the issue with those believers who are specialists. Those marketing experts who have studied and prayed about the issue more thoroughly can share their insights with the rest of us.

All of us will then be able to deal with the marketing force at work with greater understanding and be one step closer to an integrated workfaith.

Globalization

The trend toward globalization is obvious and everywhere. The world is getting smaller. Convenient worldwide communication, whether it is television, fax, computer networks, satellite transmissions or just plain old mail, is a major contributor to the "shrinking" of the world. Along with this rapid influx of global communication, there is a comparable explosion in worldwide travel. Many of us now fly to many places, and this first-hand experience of other parts of the globe minimizes narrow, provincial perspectives.

The impact of globalization on the workplace is equally pervasive. The potential customer is not just the person down the street, on the other side of town, within the state or in the nation. Potential customers are now around the globe. The same is true of potential workers. On a daily basis, workers in Taiwan, Germany, Brazil, India and the United States all contribute to a single product. Parts may come from one country, and assembled in a different country, packaged in yet another nation and distributed through a different country on another continent. The globalization of business, along with its subsequent economic interdependence, is a force at work.

Whether this trend is "good" or "bad" on economic and social grounds is debated. At the heart of the discussion is the distribution of jobs, and, therefore, the health of national economies. Jobs leaving the industrial nations and migrating to the third world and developing countries is "bad" for the industrial nations but "good" for the developing countries. The net effect is that the world is becoming more balanced in terms of job opportunities. But "more balanced" may mean less income for some groups that have been accustomed to more income while the same balance translates into a higher standard of living for people who previously lived in poverty.

The final verdict on this globalization of work is not in yet. Cheaper labor and relaxed environmental laws in some countries lead to lower production costs, and therefore higher profits. Whether this trade-off in terms of labor and the environment is worth it depends on many factors, including who is making the assessment. The fact of globalization cannot be disputed but the challenges of this same globalization are far from resolved.

The reality is that increased global economic interdependence is inevitable. This reality affects many of us directly and many others indirectly. What is the appropriate workfaith response to this trend?

Without judging the specifics of individual cases, we will support globalization in general. From a faith perspective, anything that contributes to greater unity among people and nations is progress. The assumption however is that greater unity will emerge from the globalization of work. It must be admitted that this assumption is in fact an assumption. It is possible that greater knowledge of other nationalities and more worldwide economic interdependence will lead to increased prejudice, unethical business practices that victimize people from other countries, and other forms of exploitation.

This threat is not academic and it has historical precedents. The colonialism of previous centuries created many examples of exploitation of cultures. Outright slavery, poverty-inflicting political and economic policies, and starvation wages are all too prominent on the pages of the history of colonialism. As today's world moves rapidly toward globalization, the possibility of similar practices is very real.

Therefore, we will be critical and cautious when evaluating the impact of specific examples of economic internationalization. The sins of the past must be condemned and avoided.

On the other hand, the underlying theme of globalization is compatible with our vision of a united, worldwide loving community. Admittedly, this vision is idealistic. But the idealism is rooted in the belief that all people are God's people and that genuine believers are called and challenged to contribute to the building of the global community as well as to the neighborhood community. From the viewpoint of faith, we are all interconnected by our common human nature and by the Christian belief in the universality of redemption. No race, color, culture, creed, nationality, gender, knowledge, age, strength, wealth or military clout can negate the fundamental truth of the absolute equality of all people at the level of human nature.

Our belief is that people have different levels of knowledge, skill, maturity, and opportunity, but that beneath these differences there is a more basic recognition of commonness and equality. While admitting these differences, we will also accept and respond to this common ground. All people deserve a level of respect because they are people.

We will avoid prejudices against other nationalities when the globalization of work enters our workplace directly. There may be disagreements about the wisdom and value of a specific project, but these disagreements must never degenerate into racial, ethnic or personal slurs. The belief in the essential value of each person is too critical to be ignored in any situation. But this belief does not interfere with the business decisions that we have to make. The point is that these decision are based on business concerns that also reflect the belief in the value of each human being. Contrary to the opinions of some cynics, sound business decisions and practices can be made while retaining an uncompromising commitment to the value of each person.

Globalization of the workplace can be viewed as an opportunity or a disaster. More than likely, it is both. In any case, it is inevitable. We will emphasize the opportunities in terms of the building of the world community and do what we can to minimize or correct the negative factors. Minimally we will avoid a perverted nationalism that automatically condemns foreign cultures and people. We know that all of us are created by God and deserve the essential respect that all God's creatures deserve.

Technology

Keeping up with technology is impossible. There are so many fields that fall under the label of "technology" that no one can be knowledgeable about all of them. Computers, robotics, communications, lasers, micro chips, avionics, virtual reality—welcome to the technology revolution.

This revolution impacts every workplace. There are few work procedures that are the same today as they were fifty years ago—or even ten years ago! And the rate of this techno-logical change is increasing rapidly. Computer advancements, for example, seem to occur almost daily.

There is no need to demonstrate the fact of technology and its influence on the workplace. It is obvious. What is not so obvious is what we are to do about this constant technological change from a workfaith point of view.

As with the other forces at work there is no "one way" that we must approach technology. There is room for honest dis-agreement about how a specific technological breakthrough should be applied to a particular workplace.

On the other hand, there are some principles related to technology that are compatible with workfaith and some that are not. For example, all technology is meant to be *for people*. That simple principle puts technology into perspective. It is not meant to limit research or downgrade the value of "pure science." But it does insist that at some level the value of the technology depends on its value to people. As a result, it runs contrary to the position that "what can be done, should be done." The workfaith principle states that "what can be done, should be done only if some positive value for people can be reasonably assumed." There is considerable latitude in this principle in that scientists need not know all the conse-quences of their research before they begin. In fact, often the nature of research is to discover what the consequences will be. The point of the principle is that these workfaith scientists will have some reasonable hope that the results of their exper-iments will somehow benefit people.

Believers who advance technology will have to critique their jobs just like all of us. They will have to compare the principles that are operative in their workplace with the prin-ciples and beliefs of their faith. More than likely they will dis-cover authentic compatibility much more often than conflict. When they do identify conflict, they will have to reconcile the issue with their conscience.

On the other end of the spectrum are all the workers who

"use" this ever advancing technology—workers like you and me. Many of us applaud the advances and eagerly wait for the inevitable next step. Some of us simply accept what technology offers without much reflection and take advantage of the benefits and absorb the disadvantages. For example, people who watch a lot of television may enjoy the benefits of the entertainment, information and education available to them. But they may also assume the negative consequences of less personal family interaction and the overall inability to carry on an articulate and rewarding conversation because they don't "practice" meaningful conversation often enough.

Then again there are some people who fear technology because it represents change and they simply don't want to change. They figure things are going well enough as they are now. New technology may force changes that are stressful and give no assurance that the end result will be an improvement. "New and improved" can very easily be interpreted as "threatening." This fear of technology is very real, even among people who go home and enjoy the benefits of their microwave ovens, remote control televisions, compact disk sound systems, cellular phones, and answering machines.

Some people fear technology because they see it as a threat to their job. It's true that technology has eliminated or radically changed many jobs. There's a very small demand for horse carriages these days even though, at one time, manufacturing horse carriages was a thriving business. The same is true of ice boxes, milkmen, ox plows, telegraph operators, bowling pin setters, and thousands of other jobs. The effect of "progress" is inevitable change in the workplace. Some workers are understandably worried.

Workfaith believers who use technology can be found in all three categories: those who are enthusiastic about new technology, those who are indifferent and those who fear it. However, all three groups will agree on some workfaith principles that will distinguish them from non-believers who also belong to these three groups.

For instance, we will not hesitate to claim that God is the only constant in an ever changing world of technology. This belief in the constancy of God will be present in the workplace when the newest computer or piece of machinery is brought into the office or factory. Whether we are enthusiastic, indifferent or fearful, we will rely on and refer to our faith in a constantly loving God who will not change. This faith is an anchor in our life, including our life at work. Technology is neither a savior nor a devil. God, in and through Jesus, is the only savior. And the devil is not a computer chip. Technology is a tool to accomplish a goal. When we put technology in its place, we live with it much more comfortably.

Loss of a job because of technology is certainly not easy to accept. But we can draw on our conviction that security is an illusion unless we are referring to our trust in God. As difficult as a layoff is, we have another resource we can turn to when faced with insecurity on the job. This reliance on faith in the loss of a job is not forced or artificial—not for workfaith believers. We have been aware of and responding to God's presence all along while we were at work. It is not strange or foreign, then, to be aware of and respond to Godpresence if technology forces us to lose our job.

Technology, obviously, is another of the forces at work that impact the workplace. We need to reflect on its influence in the light of faith. To do so helps us integrate our work and our faith, and offers us the opportunity to discover and respond to yet another aspect of God on the job.

Conclusion

The seven forces at work identified in this chapter—competition, women in the workplace, management and labor, regulations, marketing, globalization, and technology—are some of the ingredients in the "atmosphere" or "culture" at work. There are other forces or trends that could be considered: the aging of the workforce as the baby boomers get older, the ethnic mix of the workforce, the politics of the country and the world, etc.

Some of these forces may be very prominent in certain workplaces and not in others. Each workplace will have its own configuration and flavor, much of it filtered through the personalities of the people on the job. As workfaith believers, we will identify the forces that are present in our specific workplace as best we can, and then reflect on these forces in the light of our faith. We will share these insights and questions with other workfaith believers. Our growing awareness will sharpen our ability to discover Godpresence at work and help us integrate work and faith.

The rewards for this integration will be great because we can then find God more easily, even at work.

Study Questions

1. Describe some of the "forces at work" on your job. Are some of these forces similar to the seven outlined in this chapter? If so, how are they similar?

2. Which force in your work area is the most negative? What can you do to change that force or minimize its impact? Which force is the most positive? How can you support that force?

3. Describe Godpresence within the forces you identified on your job.

4. We often become occupied with the details of our specific, individual tasks. What is the value of reflecting on these general forces in our work environments?

5. Choose a recent current news event and identify how God was present to that event. What was God doing during the event?

6

People at Work

Almost all of us work with someone. Even some jobs that seem individualistic (freelance writer, self-employed cabinet-maker, farmer, etc.) usually depend on other people as customers, advisors or suppliers. In any case, even if there is an occasional job that is truly isolated, the vast majority of us must work with other people.

Workfaith, then, includes these relationships with co-workers. In previous chapters we considered the work activity itself and the forces that make up the overall work environment. This focus was essential in order to outline workfaith, but the relationships at work are also critical.

This personal dimension to workfaith is relatively easy to identify as potential for kingdom building. Most of us recognize that relationships with people, including people at work, are connected with faith and God's kingdom. Loving God and loving neighbor, even in the workplace, are generally accepted as appropriate faith topics. For the most part, then, the issue is not trying to prove that faith as it relates to people at work is legitimate. The more challenging aspect of this issue is the question of how this faith is experienced.

But let's not be too hasty. Some workers insist that people at work have nothing to do with faith or kingdom building. This is the position of non-believers, even non-believers who promote kindness, respect, fairness and forgiveness among all employees. They live gospel values without calling them gospel values, and their motivation for this behavior is a basic respect for humanity, a sense of the value of life, the golden rule or some other personal value that is consistent with the gospel. From a Christian perspective, these people are building the kingdom by their attitude and behavior. These workers never express this attitude in faith terms; in fact, they may explicitly reject religious references and argue against any or all faith.

Some believers also reject the faith dimension to people at work. For them, life is so segmented that work and faith have no common ground. They see no connection between relationships at work and the gospel call to love your neighbor. Hopefully, there aren't too many of these believers.

Most of us admit that our relationships at work are somehow connected with our faith. Just how this connection takes place on a daily basis is not very clear, but the general principle is widely accepted. Of course, there is great variety among believers in terms of faith maturity, scope, depth and content. Some workfaith believers automatically see all relationships everywhere, even very casual ones, as faith related. Other believers are seldom aware of relationships as associated with faith. Some people admit this connection when they consciously reflect upon it, which is seldom. Other believers make a conscious effort to include co-workers and work situations in their prayer and faith life. Therefore, even though most believers admit to the connection between faith and people at work, they certainly don't understand or live this alliance in the same way.

I mentioned a number of times that all relationships, by nature and by Christ's redemption, imitate and participate in the life of the Trinity. This imitation and participation is, of course, limited. No one can be God except God. However, God has chosen to invite us to share in God's life, and provides the means that make it possible to accept that invitation. This is one way to describe grace. Basically, grace is a theological term which describes the relationship between God and us. In its simplest terms, grace is the presence of

God. As such grace admits to varying degrees of presence, as we saw in chapter 2. Through grace, we participate in God's life, but we do so in differing degrees.

God's life is always and everywhere Trinitarian. There is no "life in the Spirit," for example, that is not also "life in the Trinity." A disciple of Jesus is automatically incorporated into the Father and the Spirit as well. To believe in God, love God, hope in God or even talk about God is always and essentially a belief, love, hope or talk about the three persons in one divine nature. Any other position would turn so-called Christians into either polytheists (believing in three separate, distinct gods) or singletarian monotheists (believing in one god who is one person, not three persons). Genuine Christians accept that when Father, Son or Holy Spirit is present, the other two must necessarily also be present.

Many of us have become accustomed to referring to Father, Son or Holy Spirit almost as if they are not a Trinity. Perhaps the mystery of the Trinity is so unimaginable that the natural tendency is to isolate the three persons and deal with them as if they were totally distinct persons without practical reference to their one divine nature. It is easy enough to fall quite innocently into this way of thinking. This approach ultimately winds up in something like "God, Inc." where the Father is chairman of the board, the Son is the chief operating officer and the Spirit is the ace troubleshooter for the company. Our limited ability to grasp the implications of a Trinitarian God can lead us to this and equally misleading images of God.

In reality, God is a Trinity and, as indicated earlier, a Trinity is a community. The reminder of the Trinity as community is one way of connecting the basic reality of God with human experience.

Characteristics of a Community

Since God is a community, let's explore the characteristics of a community. The usual caution must be made: God as community is not the same as humans as community. Obviously, God is unique and therefore the Trinitarian community is so unique that there are no perfect imitations. Beyond that, however, there are some characteristics of the divine community and the human community that are similar enough to provide further understanding for both God and us. These are the characteristics that are outlined here. There are, of course, other traits that could be explored, but the following three dimensions of community are pivotal in any community, divine or human.

Community: People Know One Another

For five years, John, George, Linda and Brian worked together in the planning group. Brian is the newest member, joining the group when Charlie retired. Their job is to forecast market trends, especially consumer interests in the company's line of products, and, of course, there's the on-going financial analysis of the possible impact on the company. As a group, they're good at their job.

But after all these years (John and George worked together for eighteen years—Linda came eight years ago), they still don't know each other very well. They do know each other's work strength—John is creative, George is good at analyzing, Linda is the number-cruncher and Brian has the computer skills—but they seldom talk about their personal lives. They're busy most of the time; there are always reports, projections, and reassesments that are due.

They do talk about ball scores, movies, TV, and some politics occasionally (usually at lunch) but they know very little about each other personally. For example, no one knows that George's dad is dying of cancer, or that Linda's husband was just promoted, or that Brian's daughter broke her arm. No one knows that John is an avid Civil War buff or that George loves fishing or that Linda is the president of her Homeowners' Association.

Is their experience exaggerated? Perhaps. How well do the people in your work group know each other? In many workplaces, there's an acceptable level of personal sharing, and

anything beyond that meets with silence or outright rejection. The level of acceptability varies, but there seem to be
major limitations on personal sharing at work.

In any true community people know one another, at least to
some extent. The neighborhood "community" may include
best friends and people who don't even recognize each other.
The word "community" should be restricted to those people
who know each other to some degree. Without this basic
knowledge, community is a worthless word. Therefore, knowing one another in community admits of degrees. In a true
community, whether it be neighborhood, family, church or
work, the people do have some knowledge of each other and
attempt to know each other better.

In the workplace, co-workers know each other, and in working together we generally get to know each other better over
time. However, this continuing knowledge is not automatic, as
the experience of the planning group demonstrates. People
can work side by side for years and reveal little more about
themselves than surface information. One worker may simply
not pay attention to co-workers and therefore, even if the co-
workers attempt to reveal more about themselves, they may
never be able to communicate this personal dimension to inat-
tentive co-workers. When this personal communication is
missing, the community aspect of people at work remains, but
it is that much less effective as a community.

In any case, whether we're good at it or not, people at
work do, in fact, know one another. In varying degrees, then,
we reflect this first characteristic of community.

This characteristic of knowing one another is also present
in the Trinity. The three persons know each other completely
because they each possess divine knowledge, but they also
know each other as distinct persons who are also united. In
fact, knowing each other is a central quality of the Trinitarian
community. Their knowledge is one, just as their nature is
one. And yet they remain distinct persons who also know
each other as distinct persons. Their knowledge is complete.

As workfaith believers, we attempt to know our co-workers. We seek ways to share our own life in ever-increasing ways and pay attention to the signals from other people about their life. The process of getting to know other people is not the same at work as it is among friends and family. While there are definite challenges in getting to know family and friends, the work environment presents an additional set of challenges. By design, getting to know family and friends is an approved part of these relationships. Personal insecurities or past history may put obstacles in the way of greater knowledge, but among family and friends the concept of increasing personal knowledge is generally accepted.

When we focus on the workplace, however, this acceptance is not very clear. At work, we are together not by choice but by accident. Or, as some believers insist, we become co-workers by God's design. In either case, the choice of co-workers is not a personal choice. We work together for eight hours a day because we all have a task to perform, a task that most often could be accomplished by a different set of people. As a result, the need to know each other is not evident.

To complicate matters even further, people at work are usually thrown together not because of personal attraction (as in the case of friendship), nor because of a common history (as is the case of families), but because we happen to work at the same place at the same time. Personalities will most likely clash. The incentive to know one another better is not there. Most of us simply want to do our job in peace. We normally treat other workers with common courtesy and expect the same in return. Most of the time this arrangement is satisfactory. But there is no motivation to know other workers in any but superficial ways.

Workfaith believers, on the other hand, seek to know co-workers more completely. We are motivated by the conviction that the workplace is, among other things, a community and that knowing one another is a critical component of any community. We also recognize that to experience a loving community is a small, but accurate, reflection of the community which by definition is love, namely God/Trinity. We do what we can to experience this community at work. This commitment includes knowing our co-workers.

Knowing our co-workers better does not mean we will like them more. Often it's true that knowing someone better means that it is easier to love that person—but not always. There is no guarantee that knowing someone will equate to liking him or her. There are some personalities that simply don't mix well, and there are some people who frankly are not very likeable, usually because they are so negative, combative or selfish.

We will not expect friendship with these people but we will always be open to learning more about them in the hope that this additional knowledge may offer us some opportunity to express our concern and care more explicitly. This desire to learn more about others cannot be forced and must not detract us from the primary purpose of the job, which is to accomplish the assigned task. Workfaith believers, then, will have the reputation as people who are interested in co-workers as persons, not just as functionaries. When we relate to others with this genuine concern and interest, we contribute to the experience of community at work, and we are doing our part to build the kingdom of the triune God in our workplace.

Community: People Respect One Another

Perhaps the reason John, George, Linda and Brian don't know each other very well is because they really don't respect each other. John is 61, George is 48, Linda is 37 and Brian is 29. They never seem to get beyond their generational differences. Besides, George is black, Linda is a quiet feminist, John is a conservative Republican and Brian is an environmentalist. These differences are seldom expressed, but they all feel them as obstacles to their personal relationships. That's just the way it is. The style was established years ago, and while new people come and go, the pattern remains. Beneath the surface of the work relationship, there's suspicion and, ultimately, a lack of basic respect for each other.

Respect means to accept another person, even in those areas where the other is different. Respect is much more than a polite nod or gentle smile. It means to pay attention, to show esteem and consideration. Basic respect is due all people because they exist. There is also the reality of *earned* respect in the sense that a person behaves in an exemplary or admirable way. While earned respect is certainly legitimate, the focus here is on something more fundamental. This basic respect reflects the conviction that all people, and in fact all creation, deserve attention, consideration and esteem because they exist.

All forms of prejudice, discrimination and hatred are sins of disrespect. When racism, agism, or sexism enter, respect leaves. When put-downs, derogatory jokes, belittling comments, ignoring others and disregard are present, respect is absent.

John, George, Linda and Brian, even when they are "civil" to each other, carry a variety of prejudices with them. The racism, agism and sexism that, in varying degrees, is present in the group makes it impossible for them to truly respect each other.

The heart of respect is the acceptance of people, and traits of people, that are different. Often the causes of disrespect are differences in color, race, history, language, physical makeup, culture, religion, sex, age or education. Unfortunately, the history of humanity can be traced by following one or a number of these areas in which people are different. Each generation, in countries around the globe, must deal with the conflicts that are caused by this inability to accept differences among various people.

Respect is so basic because it implies this acceptance of differences. It insists that all of us are fundamentally equal and deserve consideration, esteem and attention. It does not mean that people who do evil things are to be ignored or allowed to harm others. It does not mean that laws can be broken without consequences. It does not mean people should not be held accountable for their actions.

It does mean that, regardless of the action, all people deserve some level of esteem simply because they exist.

In wholesome communities, people respect one another. In fact, this respect is so essential that, without it, there is little or no chance of the community being a "good" community. Genuine communities must have some level of respect.

It's not surprising, then, that respect is also a key characteristic of the Trinity. Within the Trinity this respect is present infinitely. The Father, Son and Holy Spirit share divinity, and yet they respect their differences. The Father is not the Son and the Holy Spirit is not the Father. Their differences are profound. However these mysterious relationships interact, they are always respectful. They always esteem, admire, support and love each other. Without destroying the divine unity, they recognize, accept, applaud and celebrate their differences.

Healthy communities imitate this characteristic of the Trinity. These communities also experience respect in that people express their esteem for others. They treat others, even those who are different, with attention and consideration. There is no question that people in these communities recognize and accept the differences in other people and groups.

Sometimes we practice this basic level of respect in our family, neighborhood, church or civic group but disregard it when we go to work. The people at work are not treated with the same level of respect that we treat others. Disagreements between individuals and departments at work are inevitable, and too often there is little incentive to resolve these disagreements in a way that reflects basic respect. Animosities prevail, and even when a level of civility remains in order to do business, the underlying feeling is one of deep disrespect.

Workfaith believers approach these differences among people and departments at work from another point of view. We are not naive; we know that different people and departments have different agendas. The finance department views a project differently than the operations department. The marketing arm approaches business in one way while the technical group works from their perspective. These various viewpoints (all of which are legitimate) create conflicts. In the face of these conflicts, workfaith believers are always respectful. Even when we disagree and fight strenuously for our position, we always recognize and accept the differences in other positions. We never resort to personal attacks or forget the dignity and respect due all people.

By practicing this basic respect at work, we contribute to the experience of community. We build the kingdom and imitate the life of the Trinity. The community at work is undoubtedly an imperfect community, but every time we treat others with this basic respect, especially when others are aggressively expressing disrespect, we add a little more validity to the experience of community at work.

Community: People Serve One Another

We can't have community without service. Service implies that we take some action in supporting one another and other people. Along with knowing and respecting one another, service is vital to the life of any community.

Service points in two directions. Some community service is reserved for members of our own group. For example, people in a church serve other members by visiting them when they are in a hospital or teaching in the religious education program or being a reader during the liturgy. Other community service is directed to people outside our community. For example, people in the church donate food to the poor of the city, or get involved with social issues like peace, environment or neighborhood security.

Both directions of service are necessary for healthy communities. Internal service supports community members emotionally, spiritually and sometimes financially. External service protects the group from becoming in-bred and exclusively self-

focused. As a result, this external service performs a dual role:
it provides service to the recipients and an external mission to
the community. All communities, but especially Christian communities, if they are to imitate the Trinitarian community faith-
fully, have a clearly delineated external mission along with
their internal goals. For example, clubs that serve only their
own members are not as faithful to the basic Trinitarian model
as clubs that add the external dimension as well.

Once again, the Trinity is a model for community service,
as well as knowing one another and respecting one another.
Within the Trinity, the Father, Son and Holy Spirit are "other
directed," that is, the Father is *for* the Son and Spirit, the Son
is *for* the Father and Spirit, and the Spirit is *for* the Father and
Son. The Trinity is known as three persons in one God only
in terms of their other-directed relationships with each other.

But the three persons also go beyond themselves; there is
an external mission to their community. Their inner, communitarian life of love is opened up to others. The "opening up"
is the basic thrust which gives meaning to creation, redemption, Jesus, revelation, grace and the final coming of Christ.
The Trinitaian community of love is the impulse behind everything that exists. This community of Father, Son and Spirit is
so dynamic that, in a sense, it cannot remain self-contained.
The Trinity shares itself by creating all things and everyone,
and then continues that creative love by serving creation.

Workfaith believers, to be faithful to this service characteristic of community, seek ways to serve other people in the
workplace. This service is expressed in small ways, like common courtesies or going out of the way to offer either personal or work-related assistance. At times of crisis, perhaps a job
lay-off, or a death in the family, or a negative performance
review, we offer comfort. When the workload piles up and
deadlines are imminent, when conflicts with the boss or
other workers become unusually stressful, when the balance
sheet doesn't balance, we offer support without taking sides

in workplace squabbles and always seek to arrive at decisions and activities without compromising kindness.

This attitude leads to service. There are many little ways in which workers can serve co-workers. The specifics often vary, based on the workplace and the personalities, but all work environments are potential service areas. This service does not mean that we do other people's work, cover up for inadequacies or condone incompetence. What it does mean is that we look for appropriate ways to serve others, and once this orientation is established, opportunities are noticed. The key to service in the workplace is the commitment to *want* to serve.

Whenever we serve one another in the workplace, we move that community a little closer to the model of community, the Trinity. Even if we are unaware of this movement, it does in fact happen. Workfaith believers have the advantage of knowing that such service contributes to community at work which in turn helps build the kingdom which in turn reflects the communitarian life of the Trinity. This awareness can motivate us to greater service and encourage us when the work environment is very negative and divisive. Some workers serve their co-workers because they believe this approach makes for a pleasant work environment. That's fine. But workfaith believers add another dimension to this motivation—the work community is called to participate in and imitate the Trinity as fully as possible.

These three characteristics of community—know one another, respect one another and serve one another—offer a glimpse into the life of both the Trinitarian community and the human community. We not only recognize and accept these characteristics, we also recognize and accept the connection between the Trinitarian community and the work community. And we attempt to live these characteristics each day on the job.

Difficult Personalities

Often we are forced to work with people we simply don't like. Sometimes this dislike is the result of immature personalities or people with completely different values and interests. Sometimes the root of the conflict is jealousy, greed, fear or prejudice. Sometimes there is a specific incident which creates resentment that lasts for years. Sometimes two relatively stable, mature, basically loving people just don't like each other.

Troublesome relationships are possible in all areas of life. What is unique about work relationships is that we cannot escape them. In other areas of life—social groups, neighborhoods, clubs, even teams, we can rather easily leave and find more compatible friends.

At work, however, we are forced to work with whoever is there. The only alternative is to quit. While some choose to quit work because of these conflicts, most of us simply cannot afford to quit. Finding another job is difficult, stressful and costly. Therefore, most of us feel we have no choice but to work with the people we meet on the job. Ninety percent of those people may be very compatible, but the remaining ten percent may make the work experience extremely uncomfortable.

Workfaith believers, like all other workers, may not handle these conflicts very well. Who's at fault? The assumption here is that the fault may be on the part of the workfaith believers as well as other employees. Believers are not immune from causing and continuing unnecessary conflicts because we are not saints and are not blameless.

But the question of blame is not the issue. The point here is to identify and suggest ways that are consistent with the principles of workfaith when we deal with difficult personalities. The format is to describe various personality types which typically make life at work more difficult and to sketch a possible workfaith response to these personality types.

Poor Performer: Sue provides clerical support for a manager and two supervisors. At least, that's what she is supposed to do. She's been in the department for nine years, with a variety of specific tasks, three different managers, four supervisors and three reorganizations. Throughout all of these changes, Sue has been a consistently poor performer.

At this point, however, with almost ten years seniority, little can be done to change her performance or fire her.

She figured it out a long time ago. She learned how to look busy when necessary, exaggerate the amount of time it takes to perform tasks, take advantage of her original boss who was new to the department, and chat pleasantly with the "right" people.

But she does very little work—Just enough to get by and never any one thing that could get her fired. She talks as though she is concerned about the department's goals, but all she really cares about is how little she can do and collecting her pay check.

Some poor performers are incompetent; they simply and without fault don't know or can't do the job. Other poor performers have the basic ability to be at least adequately competent but their attitude interferes with their performance. Most poor performers seem to fit the second category, and it is this group that is the most difficult to deal with at work.

Some poor performers, like Sue, are very good at being poor performers. They do just the minimum amount of work to avoid getting fired or transferred, or they know how to cover their incompetence with the boss. Co-workers know what's going on, but bosses don't know the full extent of the scam. In time, expectations are lowered and the poor performers quietly go on for years, getting paid for minimal effort and meager performance.

Naturally, co-workers resent the poor performers. Because these co-workers are more dedicated and realize that the job has to get done, they pick up the slack caused by the poor performers. Some co-workers will complain bitterly about the injustice in workload distribution but often there is little change. The boss may not be able to motivate the poor performers into a more productive work style, because either company rules are restrictive or the boss simply can't effect the desired reform. The angry co-workers simply give up trying to change the situation and make whatever adjustments they can.

God on the Job

But the resentment remains. At times these co-workers may even confront the poor performer, and there may even be some temporary improvement, but in the long run little progress is made. The Sues of the world keep right on doing as little as possible—and getting away with it!

How do workfaith believers respond to poor performers? First of all, we will not be poor performers ourselves. Abilities, skills and knowledge vary, but we sincerely give our best effort to the job. This attitude toward work is not dependent on co-workers or other cultural forces. We do our best because we are personally committed to being a good performer. It is part of our personality and our deep convictions about our role in the workplace. We believe we are contributing to the kingdom by performing at our best level. How other people perform is immaterial to our dedication and commitment. We will always be true to our convictions, one of which is to give a full day's work for a full day's pay. It's a matter of personal justice but it goes beyond justice. It's also a matter of personal integrity.

This attitude doesn't deny that there may be conflicts with poor performers. We may even confront poor performers or make the extent of the poor performance known to the boss. These confrontations and reports will be charitable as well as honest. They will be devoid of revenge, hate or explosive anger. They will point to the problem and will have adequate objective proof, not accusations based on hearsay or reputation. We will retain basic respect for these poor performers even as we point out the difficulties the poor performance has on accomplishing the goals of the job. We know and honor the line between personal attack and performance critique.

If the problem with poor performers is not adequately resolved through the means available within the rules of the workplace, we will not harbor long-term resentments. In Sue's case, for example, there's no point arguing with her, complaining about her incessantly or plotting one scheme after another to improve her performance. If the proper channels don't produce results, workfaith believers will let the problem go emotionally, accept the situation as it is and continue to concentrate on our commitment to doing a superior job ourselves. We will not allow poor performers to take further advantage of us but we will get on with our work without undue anger or resentment.

Other co-workers may remain angry, resentful and revengeful toward the poor performers. And these feelings may be very understandable and possibly even justified, but we will be different. We will recognize and accept the fact that these continuing feelings interfere with our commitment and ability to build the kingdom at work, a kingdom founded on the principles of the gospel and reflective of the Trinitarian community.

Power Seekers: Engineering always fascinated Greg, so he got his degree and was hired at a small manufacturing company. His hiring manager was impressed with Greg's desire to succeed and his ambition.

At the time, his manager wasn't aware that Greg's "ambition" was really a deep-seated need to control people and events. In a word, Greg is power-hungry. He is friendly enough but it didn't take long for his co-workers to discover that his friendliness is a means to position himself for greater influence with the boss. He tries to dominate problem-solving meetings by arguing incessantly for his point of view. He visits frequently with the boss, attempting to establish a relationship that will be valuable when a promotion or raise comes along.

The workplace is fertile ground for power seekers like Greg. Power seekers are people who like to run things, make decisions, determine plans, give orders, critique performances, and expect compliance. These functions are necessary in the workplace—decisions have to be made, plans developed, tasks assigned, performance monitored and goals evaluated. Power seekers are those people who either do, or want to do, some or all of these functions. They are over-ambitious and use almost any means to achieve their personal goals.

In one sense, power and power seeking is not "bad." Often the assumption is that power is bad in itself, and therefore people who seek power are also "bad." This assumption is off-base. There is positive and negative power. Positive power refers to those people who are willing to accept the challenge of leadership, make necessary decisions, motivate people to agree with and carry out stated goals, accept responsibility for the project or position, are accountable for progress and coordinate multiple activities. Positive power usually leads to a positive workplace atmosphere.

The positive power can be exercised in many ways. Recently, the emphasis has been on sharing power with employees. The basic concept is participative management, which maintains that everyone in the company or organization has the opportunity to participate in making plans and decisions that affect the product or service the company provides. This participation may center on specific areas or it may encompass the whole work experience. Power is shared, along with responsibility, accountability and a sense of ownership.

But even in these situations, there is usually someone or some group who oversees the total process and who either accepts or rejects the recommendations that come from the whole workforce. This environment provides more opportunities for positive power seekers and encourages employees to take advantage of this diffusion of power.

In other work environments, much of this power resides in one or a few people. Other employees are expected to implement the plans and directives of these decision makers. In itself this work environment is not "bad." In fact, in some positions, the military for example, the concentration of decision making in a few people is necessary for the safety and effectiveness of the operation. Obviously inefficiency would paralyze an activity if everyone decided everything.

Positive power can exist in either a participative or a restrictive work environment. Each approach needs a different kind of leader and a different set of skills, but power can be exercised in a positive way in either setting.

Usually the power problems in the workplace are associated with negative power. Negative power implies that people use or want power for purposes other than the efficient and effective operation of the company or organization. The usual motivation behind negative power is personal. For a variety of psychological and social reasons some people seek power in order to feel superior to others. They enjoy the sense of importance they feel when they tell other people what to do, and they relish the opportunity to make other people depend on them. Another side of negative power seekers is the tendency to resent anyone who has a position of authority over them. In its purest form, then, negative power seekers enjoy controlling others and hate taking orders from others. Greg's co-workers picked up on this attitude quickly, and resented him for it. The morale in the group went downhill, and both productivity and creativity followed right behind.

Sometimes a negative power seeker, because of some other skills and an unusual amount of determination, becomes a boss. When these personalities achieve a position of authority, they often become very authoritarian. In some authoritarian organizations, this combination of negative power and position of authority works rather well. But increasingly, both in business and in government, this style of authority is becoming less productive and popular. In general, people are becoming more democratic and participative. Family life and school life are more participative in terms of authority than they were twenty-five years ago. As a result, people enter the workforce expecting a more participative experience, and, in reality, that's the only approach they know, practically speaking. When they work for a boss who is authoritarian, the predictable conflict is deep-seated and probably unresolvable.

Negative power seeking, then, has many dimensions. When negative power seekers are in a position of authority, they often become "kingdom-builders." That choice of phrase is

ironic in that genuine workfaith believers are in fact attempting to build God's kingdom in the workplace. Negative power
seekers attempt to build their own kingdom, that is, they seek
personal power and recognition. They want credit for the
accomplishments of the group in order to promote their own
career, earn more money, and/or receive recognition. Workfaith believers build God's kingdom, based on love, respect,
integrity, and acceptance of the presence of God at work.

How do we deal with Greg and other workplace power
seekers? First of all, we remind ourselves of the distinction
between the person and the person's actions. We always
respect the basic dignity of the person. On the other hand,
we are not naive; we are not easily fooled by the manipula-
tions of the negative power seekers.

Greg often develops schemes that will put him in positions
of power when it is not in the best interest of the company.
We must speak out kindly but firmly that the proposed
scheme is not the best plan, and that an alternative approach
will serve the organization better. We keep the goals of the
organization, the tasks to be accomplished and the primary
functions of the job in the forefront. Negative power seekers
undermine these goals by putting their own personal ambi-
tions ahead of the work goals. Workfaith believers insist on
achieving the goals of the workplace.

Conflicts with negative power seekers is inevitable, but we
will not enter into extended squabbles over power. We state
our position as cogently as possible, make sure that our perceptions are understood and then let it go. If decisions are
made that we disagree with, we do not harbor resentments.
We simply do our job to the best of our ability and leave the
matters that are beyond our control to the responsibility of
those who have that responsibility.

We can accept this situation because we know that the
community at work is imperfect and will always remain so.
We continue to do what we can to improve the work community by knowing others, respecting others and serving others,

but we recognize that we alone are not responsible for the work community. We know our limitations as well as our contributions. And we are at peace with the level of community we experience at work. That includes coming to terms with Greg, even if there is little hope that he will change.

This attitude is not fatalistic. It is realistic. Being at peace with the level of community at work does not mean that we give up attempting to know, respect and serve others at work. It simply means that while we do what we can, we don't operate from a basis of unrealistic expectations. If negative power seekers maneuver their way into official or unofficial positions of authority, we will maintain our integrity and do the best we can.

As workfaith believers, we also include our work community in our prayers. With the cultural separation between work and faith, it is very possible that we neglect to pray for our co-workers and our jobs in general. It follows, however, that if the workplace is truly a place where Godpresence is operative and the people at work form an automatic community reflecting the Trinity, then prayer for that community and that job is not only appropriate but required. This prayer will include all the dimensions of the workplace—the job itself, the product/service provided, the people, and even Greg.

The Gossip: With Helen it has always been that way. She just loves to talk about other people. She really isn't aware of it as a problem, even though her former friend, Joan, confronted her with it about two years ago. After a few attempts at being subtle, Joan finally became very direct.

"Helen," she said, "you just talk about other people too much. You look for little signs and then you jump to conclusions and make up things about people. And then you tell everyone."

Helen was hurt. She wasn't *that* bad, and everyone else does about the same thing, don't they? Besides, that's what keeps life interesting. After the conversation with Joan, their friendship began to cool, and before long they simply stopped contacting each other very often.

And Helen keeps on talking about other people. Doesn't everyone?

Every workplace seems to have at least one gossip. Gossips are people who listen for and repeat any and all information they can discover—or invent!—about other people. They have a need to talk about people, speculate on their motivations, and interpret actions or events from a negative point of view. Once they hear something, they immediately must tell someone else, usually with some added tidbits.

Since they are so prevalent, it isn't necessary to describe their behavior in detail. We all know! Their gossip is generally disruptive, even when they have willing ears for their many tales. Their talk undermines morale in the workplace and, from a workfaith perspective, it interferes with developing the respect needed to promote a sense of community at work.

Workfaith believers, of course, are not gossips. We respect confidential information and we do not interpret other people's motives. We stick with objective facts and speculate on other aspects of a work problem or personality only when it is necessary to make workplace decisions. We have the reputation of treating everyone fairly and are never suspected of backbiting or jealousy.

Dealing with the workplace gossip is not easy. Part of the problem is that most of us are curious about other people and work events. Gossips count on that curiosity, and feed it, probably because it makes them feel important. Workfaith believers control that curiosity, and attempt to sift out the likely truth from the embellishments. This process of discernment is difficult, and learning how to filter each gossip's tales comes only with practice, and trial and error. But this discernment and filtering is precisely what we must do in order to avoid participating in the destructive behavior of the gossip.

Speculation about the future of the company, the possible reorganization of a department or the impact of the economy on business is not gossip. Some of this speculation may even be necessary in order to prepare people emotionally for future directions the workplace may take. Gossip is generally more personal; it is about people and what they have done, may have done or will possibly do. Gossip pretends to know something others don't know about people.

Workfaith believers simply do not gossip, and when we have to listen to some gossip because it is unavoidable, we do not repeat it or even believe it. At times we ask questions or make statements that indicate we do not believe the story. We always attempt to identify the truth and discard the embellishments. We all know that not all the truth is worth repeating or even knowing. Personal matters of a scandalous or shocking nature are often no one's business in the workplace, and we will consistently honor that principle.

The best way to minimize the activity of a gossip is to encourage open communication within the workplace. When accurate information is consistently communicated, the gossip has less data to manufacture. When we know what's going on from official sources, the gossips are reduced to fabricating information or attempting to make peripheral issues sound more significant. Good workplace communication combined with a cold shoulder when the gossip starts telling stories is the best way to keep the destructive impact of the gossip in check.

The Negativist: Lou's reputation at work is mixed. Everyone knows that, as an accountant, he is excellent. His reports are always clear, to the point and well-founded. Other accountants in the office often ask him for advice and he gives it, but it is usually accompanied by some kind of insult. Sometimes it's disguised as a joke and sometimes it's more blunt. In any case, Lou's reputation as a negative person is widespread.

Nothing is ever good enough for him. A profitable quarter is not profitable enough. A new computer program won't work as well as the old one, which also has its flaws. The weather is either too cold, too hot, too rainy or too sunny. The traffic is always too hectic. His bosses are just plain dumb. People in the other departments don't know what they're doing. Life is generally unfair and "you have to fight for what you want." And his negativism is so ingrained, he doesn't even realize how pervasive it is.

It is extremely difficult to work with someone who is always negative. People who constantly find something wrong with a plan, an activity, a person or the world in general drain the joy, pride and sense of community out of the people around them. Workers who see nothing but the positive side of events are a problem also, but it seems there are many more negativists than there are unwarranted optimists.

Hopefully, most of us are realistic enough to recognize both the accomplishments and the problems within the workplace. Hopefully, we see the positive as well as the negative sides to co-workers. Hopefully, we have a relatively balanced view of the world—grateful for the benefits and opportunities we have as well as critical of the inadequacies present in society and in the workplace.

The negativists, on the other hand, react only to what is wrong. They don't help to change things for the better because, to them, there is always something wrong with the plan for improvement and/or the people involved with implementing the change. Why these people are so negative is open for debate: perhaps they have very low self-esteem and project their self-view onto the rest of the world; maybe they figure the world owes them happiness, and since they don't experience personal happiness, they blame everyone else for their unhappiness; perhaps they had a bad experience, a tragedy or a rotten deal at work and they will never let go of the pain, and therefore attack everyone and everything around them. There may be as many reasons as there are negativists. Whatever the reason, they are disruptive in the workplace.

Workfaith believers will never be negativists. We are rooted in the conviction that Jesus has overcome sin in all its forms by means of his life, death, and resurrection. We also believe that the kingdom of God is alive and well in the midst of the world, and that in the end this kingdom will triumph. This belief is not left at the office door or the factory gates. We know that the workplace, too, is included in the redemptive process of Jesus' death and resurrection. As a result of these basic convictions about the nature of life and death, we are fundamentally optimistic about life and work.

This optimism is not blind. We are very aware of the negative side of life and work. We know that people are sinners, make mistakes, are selfish and proud and greedy and lustful and envious and on and on. We know that the workplace is limited, has poorly arranged priorities, cumbersome policies and procedures, and incompetent workers. We know that things should and perhaps can be better. We see the negative side of reality as clearly as the negativists. But we see more than the negative; we also see the redemptive, the positive side of reality. We see what the negativists refuse to see.

In dealing with Lou and people with similar negative attitudes, we must never allow ourselves to be drawn into their viewpoint. We may agree with parts of their commentary but there will never be basic agreement between genuine believers and the negativists. Our fundamental perceptions are diametrically opposed.

This opposition need not be argumentative or uncharitable. When negativists make their predictable and disparaging comments, we can either ignore them or make some more positive observation. It is helpful to recall a basic rule for successful communication when dealing with negativists: when you agree with someone, let that person know that you agree; when you agree and disagree, state the area of agreement first; when you disagree, admit that you may be wrong. This formula is valid in all occasions but is particularly valuable when trying to work with people like Lou.

In any case, the primary issue is to stay focused on the basic optimism that is inherent in Christianity. In certain circumstances, short-term pessimism may be realistic. But we must be long-term optimists. And this long-term optimism has a profound impact on the present because it provides the necessary foundation for all of life, including life at work.

In the long haul, working side by side with Lou may be the most difficult working situation we will face. Adjustments can be made to policies and procedures, adaptations can be made regarding other personality types, personnel changes can be engineered to combat poor performers, powers seekers or gossips, but working with a negativist is a relentless and often subtle attack on anything positive and life supporting in the workplace. We will have to identify this problem and stay alert to the positive aspects of the job. Periodic "reality checks" are in order as well as regular reminders about the contribution our job is making to build the kingdom. Without this consistent renewal, we run the risk of inheriting the basic pessimism of our negativistic co-worker.

We will retain our fundamental optimism regardless of the attitude of our co-workers. Patience and charity are the cornerstones of our approach to negativists. But we will never comply with the pessimists.

Bosses

Obviously, some of the most influential people at work are the bosses. They set the tone, enforce the policies, evaluate performances, establish priorities, resolve conflicts and oversee the day to day progress toward production or service goals. Depending on the nature of the work, bosses come with many titles. In a large company, the immediate boss for most of us is a supervisor, foreman, or crew chief. In smaller organizations, the immediate boss may be a manager or a vice-president. In any case, unless you're the president of the company or the chief operating officer, everyone has at least one boss.

Most bosses, then, also have a boss. These people have to look both ways. We must lead and motivate the employees who report to us, and we must perform adequately for our boss or bosses. Supervisors, for example, must ensure acceptable productivity from their crew as well as enforce the directives from the managers.

There are many ways to be a boss. One extreme is the absolute authoritarian, where workers do only what they are told because they are told to do it. The other extreme is the boss who is directionless, doesn't make decisions or is simply incompetent.

Between these two extremes are multiple variations, perhaps as many as there are bosses. Principles may be the same but the specific exercise of those principles is conditioned by the personality of each boss.

Because of this variety and because being a boss is so connected with personality, it is almost impossible to describe the "perfect boss." Different workers will describe different and sometimes contradictory characteristics. Some of us want a strong, decisive supervisor; others want someone who develops consensus among the workforce before a decision is made. Some of us want regular feedback and recognition from the boss while others prefer to be left alone and find too much external recognition as demeaning. The variations go on and on, and the search for the perfect boss becomes more elusive.

The question of authority is critical. What is the role of authority in the workplace? How do we, as workfaith believers, respond to that role? St. Paul, in his letter to the Ephesians (6:5-9) and again in his letter to the Colossians (3:22-25), offers some guidance on these questions. While there are obvious differences between his culture and ours, and even though the immediate context refers to the relationship between slaves and masters, there are some principles in Paul's letters that are certainly applicable to us.

The letter to the Ephesians reads this way: "Slaves, obey your human masters with the reverence, the awe, and the sincerity you owe to Christ. Do not render service for appearance only and to please men, but do God's will with your whole heart as slaves of Christ. Give your service willingly, doing it for the Lord rather than men. You know that each one, whether slave or free, will be repaid by the Lord for whatever good he does. Masters, act in a similar way toward your slaves. Stop threatening them. Remember that you and they have a master in heaven who plays no favorites."

This teaching of Paul is not meant to condone or condemn slavery. His focus is the final verse: both slaves and masters are accountable to the same all-just and all-loving God. Paul insists that work and social relations here on earth are part of a larger reality. What Paul is describing is similar to the work-faith perspective that is the central theme of this book. Paul says that the surface relationships between slaves and masters is contained within the broader and more basic relationship between God and us. That's precisely the point of workfaith: God is present even at work, and we are challenged to recognize, accept and promote that presence in the workplace.

More precisely, Paul teaches that authority is an acceptable and even necessary part of the relationships at work. Workers are to respect authority because the bosses also represent Christ. But the other side of the coin is equally true and necessary, namely that bosses must treat their employees with respect because the employees too represent Christ. The relationships as defined at work are not the final relationships, nor even the most important definitions. Always and everywhere, all of us are subject to God, and that ultimate subjection supersedes all other relationships. This awareness colors the way we relate to our bosses and, if we are bosses, the way we relate to our employees.

Practically speaking, then, we are expected to comply with the directives of our bosses as long as these directives don't contradict the moral teachings of the gospel. By the same token, bosses are expected to treat employees with respect and never ask them to do anything that contradicts the moral teachings of the gospel.

Many of the conflicts in the workplace related to bosses and authority stem from an inadequate understanding and appreciation of the role of authority on the job. Bosses who enjoy controlling people usually get into trouble when they give orders just for the sake of forcing people to do their will. These bosses then resort to "letting them know who's boss around here."

Workfaith bosses do not resort to such power moves; it isn't important to them to demonstrate their authority because they accept that their authority is limited. They give orders and expect compliance because the nature of the job requires it, not because they enjoy making people comply with their wishes. Ultimately, these bosses earn additional respect from most of their employees.

Employees also have problems with authority, even legitimate authority that is used properly. These employees resent anyone telling them what to do. They may comply because they fear losing their job or a raise, but they are regularly angry because of their resentment. They reject even a boss who treats them with respect but who expects them to perform at an appropriate level. Employees with this exaggerated rejection of authority figures clearly have a personality problem. The fact remains, however, that in varying degrees employees with this mindset are found throughout the workplace.

Whether we are bosses or co-workers, we must work with these anti-authoritarian employees. As always we must treat these workers with respect. But we will not approve of the anti-authoritarian attitude. Workfaith implies an acceptance of authority. When this authority is misused by trying to force policies or activities that clearly violate the gospel, or when people in authority misuse the position for their own advantage, we will object and courageously identify the misuse and suggest proper remedies. Throughout this conflict, we must never undermine the legitimate use of authority. It will always be clear that authority has a needed and rightful place on the job.

This appropriate authority can be exercised in many ways. The current approach is to include all levels of employees in some form of consultation and decision making role. Some of us enthusiastically support this approach while others support a more traditional approach. From a workfaith perspective, this debate over the specifics of how the workplace should be organized and how the authority should be divided is not the basic issue. Workfaith simply asserts that authority is somehow present and needs to be accepted, and that all of us, bosses and employees alike, must treat each other with love and respect.

This love and respect is possible regardless of the specific workplace structure. After all, the work community is a small imitation of the Triune community which is based on divine communitarian love. When we improve the level of love and respect within the workplace, we reflect the presence of God. Authority does not interfere with this presence, but the misuse of authority on either the bosses' part or the employees' part will sabotage the workfaith community.

Bosses, then, are an integral part of the work community. They are also an integral part of the workfaith community and must be included in any attempt to describe this community. Though their functions may vary, and though we may be held accountable for the success or failure of the project or work assignment, we must always try to love and respect co-workers, regardless of their position.

Man-Woman Relationships at Work

The workplace is a confusing myriad of interrelationships. Family counselors and theorists have concluded that the family is system, that is, the whole is greater than the sum of the parts. There is more to family than adding up the relationships of all of the members. If any one member has a problem or makes a change, it affects the whole system. If one member needs special care, the other members may also need some care. It is often beneficial, then, to deal with the whole family system as well as the individual members of that family.

The workplace is similar, although the social and emotional

studies have not been done on the workplace as they have on the family. While the relationships at work are usually not as personal and intimate as they are in the family, there is enough similarity between work and family relationships to warrant the basic comparison.

Workplace relationships are also a system. The whole is greater than the sum of the parts, and what happens to one worker generally has some impact on the rest of the workers. When one worker retires, quits or dies, and is replaced by a new worker, the network of relationships is changed, sometimes slightly and sometimes profoundly.

Most of the commentary on workplace relationships revolves around productivity issues. The implication in these studies is that the workers are functionaries—with tasks to be accomplished, and the focus is on what it takes to motivate workers to produce at ever increasing rates. This focus is not automatically demeaning. In fact, many of the current efforts to improve productivity are based on the conviction that treating employees with respect will motivate them to produce more. Humane treatment is in the best interest of the company or organization. Besides, a growing body of law protects employees from mistreatment in more and more areas. The net result is that life in the workforce is generally more humane than it was in the past.

But even that improved status is based on one thing: increased productivity. The bottom line is that workers are fundamentally viewed as functionaries, human functionaries to be sure, but functionaries nonetheless.

An analysis of workplace relationships that centers on workers exclusively as people would be very helpful. The conclusions would likely parallel the findings regarding the family. There are definite differences between family and work relationships but there are also similarities. After all, many of us actually spend more time interacting with our co-workers than with our family.

Within the system of relationships at work, there are many sub-systems. In a large organization, these sub-systems continue to multiply. In a small business, they are confined to a few people. Each experience has advantages and disadvantages: in a large setting, there are more choices for finding compatible relationships, but each person can get "lost" in the numbers. In a small business the relationships are more personal but there are fewer choices for relationships. In any case, personal relationships at work are an inevitable part of the job, and, as such, they are an integral part of workfaith.

Relationships between men and women at work are one of the major subsystems affecting people at work. In Chapter 5 on the "Forces at Work" we saw how "women in the workplace" are a major trend affecting the experience of work. In this chapter, we will take a closer look at the relationships between men and women in the workplace. Since these relationships are so prevalent, and changing, it is essential that we view them from a workfaith perspective.

The fact that more women are entering the workforce; that the societal, familial and work related roles of men and women are changing; that women are achieving positions of workplace leadership previously reserved for men; that men and women now relate differently in the workplace than a few decades ago; that this explosion of changing roles will continue—all these facts have been documented and, more importantly, experienced by millions of workers.

We are called to contribute to the kingdom of God by developing a community at work by knowing, respecting and serving other people, as I described earlier in this chapter. Since these characteristics of community are so fundamental and vital both to the Trinitarian and the human community, I will refer to them again as we look more closely at man-woman relationships at work.

Man-Woman Relationships at Work: Knowing One Another

Man-woman relationships at work can be both professional and personal—simultaneously. Knowing one another professionally means that we recognize the particular expertise of the other person and we count on that knowledge and skill to accomplish a task. Knowing one another personally means that we know something about the personality of the other, the emotional makeup, the likes and dislikes, and basic personal facts, for example, family status and health conditions.

For the purpose of the job, it is not necessary to know other people personally. The only requirement is to know the skills and functions of co-workers. For the purpose of work-faith community, however, it is necessary to know something of the personal life of co-workers.

We will, therefore, attempt to be personal on the job. But there are dangers, especially when man-woman relationships are involved. Being too personal, even with same sex relationships, can interfere with job productivity. Too much personal conversation simply cuts away at time needed to perform adequately. Getting to know co-workers can be an excuse for laziness and lack of responsibility. Extended and frequent coffee breaks with co-workers, lunch hours that exceed company policies, prolonged informal visits about hobbies, personal interests or family matters, lengthy debates about news events— all may promote personal relationships but at the expense of professional responsibilities. Workfaith believers will not use these methods to get to know co-workers. We promote this dimension of community but we keep it within acceptable boundaries in terms of time spent visiting with co-workers.

Man-woman relationships at work are complicated. The complications become dangerous depending on the man and/ or woman involved. At times, man-woman relationships at work turn into romance which leads to marriage. Sometimes these marriages are long-lasting and wonderful. The spouses continue to work for the same company, sometimes even in the same department, and everything turns out fine both at home and at work. Workplace romances are not automatically sordid. In fact. since people spend a lot of time on the job, the workplace is a predictable arena for people to meet, fall in love and get married.

On the other hand, the workplace can also lead to destructive man-woman relationships. If you are seeking an extra-marital affair, you can often find a willing partner at work. If you are seeking comfort or escape from a marriage, but not wanting a sexual relationship, you can usually find this level of support at work also. A single person seeking temporary intimate relationships will probably find someone at work who is willing to cooperate. In general, the workplace can be a fertile ground for finding whatever level of relationship you may want. It may take courage and ingenuity to discover willing partners, and it is more likely that you'll find this partner in larger organizations, but the opportunities exist and some people take advantage of these opportunities.

Workfaith believers will be personal with members of the opposite sex. But we will know and honor limits. We will not incorporate or imply overtly sexual matters into the conversation. In a broad sense, man-woman relationships, like all relationships, are inherently sexual. We appreciate this basic sexuality but we do not exploit or demean this sexuality. We do not have hidden agendas or motivations. We are personal but with no other intention than to be personal. We do not accept stereotypes of what men and women are—or should be. We respond to each co-worker as an individual, and attempt to know that person as an individual. The purpose of the personal relationship is to get to know the other person better in order to respect and serve that person better. Using this approach and keeping within the appropriate limits, we know our co-workers personally and thereby help build the sense of community at work.

There are some people who don't want to be known personally. They prefer to keep their personal life and their work life separate. In these situations, we honor the wishes of these people and maintain a friendly, personal attitude toward them. The fact that these people choose, for whatever reason, to be more guarded personally is no reason why we can't remain open and pleasant to them.

It is possible, then, for us to know co-workers personally. Go as far as limits allow in getting to know co-workers. The limits are determined by workplace conditions, the willingness of other people, and self-imposed boundaries. The combination of limits will vary with different co-workers. There are no absolute rules, beyond the principles of basic morality, that govern these relationships. We walk the fine line between being personal and "going too far."

Man-Woman Relationships at Work: Respecting One Another

The greatest hindrance to man-woman respect is stereotypes. If men view women as fundamentally unable to compete in the workplace, then these men do not respect female co-workers. If women view men as fundamentally insensitive, then these women do not respect male co-workers. If men think of women primarily as sex objects, then these men do not hold women in high esteem. If women think of men primarily as wage-earners, then these women show little personal consideration for men. If men see women as capable of performing only certain traditional jobs, then these men do not support women who achieve non-traditional positions. If women see men as unable to do presumed female tasks, then these women do not respect the men who in fact do these tasks.

The list goes on. Stereotypes rob people of respect. And respect is one of the characteristics that contribute to healthy communities, including the community at work.

We need to honestly examine ourselves in terms of the stereotypes we may have regarding co-workers of the opposite sex. Man-women workfaith relationships must be built on respect. In order to develop this respect, we must look closely at our feelings and determine if they have consciously or subconsciously assumed some of the cultural gender-related stereotypes. Most of us have probably inherited some of these assumptions.

To root out these unfair and unchallenged presuppositions, we may have to talk with others about these prejudices. A small group of supportive friends can be helpful. Perhaps one other trusted person can provide the necessary mirror for us to identify their stereotypes. These assumptions are so ingrained that it is difficult, even for sincere workfaith believers, to identify our prejudices honestly and develop a method to change them. Many of these stereotypes are habits, mindsets that have been accepted for years, and they don't go away quickly or easily. Other people can be an invaluable aid for those of us who want to rid ourselves of these stereotypes.

However it is done, it is essential that we eliminate these prejudices in order to treat other people with the respect needed to build a Trinitarian-like community at work. Prejudice is not limited to men-women relationships but it is an area where prejudice is evident and widespread. It needs attention if we are going to contribute to the growth of the kingdom of God at work.

Man-Woman Relationships at Work:
Serving One Another

Within the context of man-woman relationships, how can we serve one another at work? First of all, we can be honest with one another. If we know and respect one another, we have a basis to talk with each other without the interference of stereotypes or hidden motivations. We can share our fears and joys, hopes and disappointments without the complications of unknown expectations or the suspicion that he or she wants "more out of the relationship." We can simply be friends and friendly.

Secondly, we can serve one another by being role models of the opposite sex. Probably we spend the most time with members of the opposite sex at work than in any other setting except family. This work setting is a valuable opportunity for all of us to experience wholesome gender relationships. It is a prime method to counteract the stereotypes we have. We serve one another, and the rest of the workforce, by consistently and clearly avoiding the stereotypes and by continually being honest with everyone. It is a great service to members of the opposite sex to lovingly remind them, by word and action, that gender prejudices limit all of us. Without condescension or pride, we serve the community at work by expanding the possibilities of how men and women relate both professionally and personally.

Conclusion

People at work are unquestionably an essential component of workfaith. Along with the work activity itself and the forces at work, people at work make up the "raw material" of workfaith. Whether we know it or not, whether we do it well or not, we are a community. And all communities imitate and, in varying degrees, share in the life of the Trinitarian community. We attempt to improve this experience of community at work by continually getting to know, respect and serve co-workers better, even those workers who have character defects like the poor performers, power seekers, gossips and negativists. This attempt to build community also includes the bosses and extends into difficult areas like the changing circumstances involving man-woman relationships.

We can integrate the total work experience with our faith. The work activity, the forces at work, and the people at work all combine to create a total work experience. Faith can be a part of this experience because God is actively present in the whole experience as well as in its various components. As workfaith believers, we recognize, accept, support, promote and celebrate this Godpresence.

Study Questions

1. There are many ways to think about the mystery of the Trinity. Is the Trinity-as-Community an approach that you find spiritually enriching? If so, how? If not, which approach to the Trinity do you find enriching?

2. *This chapter identifies three key elements of community—knowing, respecting and serving one another. What are other elements of community that you have experienced? Can these elements also be experienced at work?*

3. *Which of the "difficult personalities" in this chapter do you find most annoying on your job? Are there other types of difficult personalities at your work? If so, describe them. What is a good workfaith response to these troublesome co-workers?*

4. *Describe the type of authority used by the bosses in your work area. What is a workfaith response to your bosses and their type of authority?*

5. *Discuss the man-woman relationships in your workplace. How well do these relationships measure up to the characteristics described in this chapter? From a workfaith perspective, how can these relationships be improved?*

7

Love That Profit!

Jeff and Brenda work in a plant that manufactures air compressors. Their group is responsible for inventory control. They order and keep track of all the parts needed to make the compressors, and they make sure that the finished products are shipped to customers. They like their jobs and their group.

But they have a fundamental difference. Their disagreement does not cause any major conflicts because they both want to avoid too much overt tension. They are friendly to each other, and they work together very well. The job demands efficiency and they both are efficient.

Jeff believes that the bottom line is profit. He works, and expects others to work, so that the company makes money, and he keeps his job. Other factors are significant only in that they directly impact the bottom line. He is motivated by measurable goals and the hope of meeting those goals.

Brenda agrees that the company needs to make a profit. But making profits doesn't really motivate her. She believes that, as a practical matter, teamwork and a feeling of acceptance, friendliness and concern for each other are more important than a preoccupation with profits. She promotes social gatherings for the group and their families, office birthday parties and a departmental bowling team. She says it's essential that the group feels good about each other and that efficiency and profits will be a by-product of these positive feelings. Jeff thinks she is too concerned about "fluff" but he is the anchor on the bowling team and eats the biggest piece of birthday cake.

Their diverse philosophies of work illustrate the tension between making a profit and nurturing a loving community at work. Like Jeff, many people maintain that, in the final analysis, there is no tension between people and profits because the workplace is not *intended* to be a loving community. The purpose of the workplace is to make a profit or to provide a service, as is the case with tax-funded government agencies. If co-workers also learn to "love" one another, then that's a bonus, but it certainly isn't the purpose of the workplace.

Love at Work

Terminology here is very important. Many people reject the concept of a "loving community" when applied to work. That terminology is too "churchy." But many of these same people, and companies, promote friendly, helping, supportive, caring relationships with co-workers. These same people express concern about a co-worker's sick child, willingly help out on a difficult assignment, visit amiably over lunch, and simply enjoy being with co-workers for eight hours a day. Many of us identify with these specific behaviors; in fact, we try to live them every day. Companies promote these kinds of relationships by sponsoring programs based on respect for all people and the need to communicate more effectively.

What else is this but elements of a "loving community"? Is it a perfect community? No, not at all! Are there probably people at work who are hard to love or even like? Yes, of course!

But who says the loving community has to be perfect? Loving communities are not limited to church groups, support groups, families and friends. There are all kinds of loving communities identified by many different names. Clubs, teams, neighborhood associations, civic groups, gangs, societies, etc.—in varying degrees they are all loving communities. Some are better at it than others but essentially all gatherings are, at their deepest level, love gatherings. Some of these gatherings do a very poor job of loving either themselves or other people. Some of these groups do pretty well at loving even when they don't identify it or consciously attempt to do it.

Even when the primary purpose of the group is to do something else, such as build a bridge, paint a house, make a decision, or win a game, the unnamed purpose of the group is to love. Human nature has so decreed. That's how we are made; that's what we are inevitably destined to do. At the level of nature, to love is the definition of existence. With God, this identification of love with essence and existence is complete and perfect. With us, this identification is far from perfect. We are capable of extreme selfishness, paralyzing fear, overwhelming anger, self-defeating insecurities and deep-seated hostility. But even in the worst case, we are still made to love. That is our innate calling; that is our final destiny. Whether we achieve this destiny is not the issue right now. The fact is we are all created in order to love, and when we gather we become a loving community.

At work, then, we automatically form a loving community. The terminology may not be acceptable in the workplace. Substitute expressions may be more acceptable, phrases like "we get along together pretty well at work" or "I like most of the people in my group at work," or even negatively when we say "the atmosphere at work is terrible right now." However it is labeled, the references to work relationships are seldom considered a "loving community."

That's fine! There's no point trying to change all those labels. On the other hand, it is important for believers to view what we experience daily through the eyes of faith. Using the term "loving community" is one way to refocus. From a faith perspective, loving community is an absolutely legitimate way to think about and talk about relationships at work. From a faith perspective, all gatherings of people create loving communities. The only issue is how well or poorly we do it. We see this connection and share this perspective, and we attempt to make the community more obviously loving.

The tension between Jeff and Brenda, between profit and people, is real. Are these two forces mutually exclusive? No! In some work settings they are obviously and successfully combined. On the other hand, there are work situations where they are obviously not combined. To many people like Jeff, profit is the reason for work and love gets in the way. Love, therefore, is not only inappropriate, it is interruptive.

There is some validity to this opinion. To neglect the profit motive leads to unemployment. There is no argument that will counteract the basic fact that if a company consistently loses money and has no source of revenue, that company cannot continue solely on the basis of the loving community the employees have formed, even when the community includes the president and officers of the company. The economic reality is simple: without profits the company must close.

By the same token, to neglect the love motive leads to employee dissatisfaction, greed, and disregard for basic human needs. The tension between people and profit remains.

Love at work. That's not the title of a racy movie or a mindless sit-com. It's a challenge. Living with the tension creatively means that we accept the validity of both poles, that we are motivated by both the need for profit and the desire for a loving community. We use our talent, knowledge and skill to contribute as much as possible to the profit goals of our company or department. At the same time, we relate to our co-workers with the conscious desire to create and nourish a sense of community: caring, understanding, acceptance, respect and forgiveness. As we attempt to create this kind of work environment, we are aware that we are building a loving community. We may never talk about it at work, but we know what we are doing and why we are doing it.

Profit,—At All Cost?

In a practical manner, it is difficult at times to combine the profit motive with concerns for people. This tension shows up most dramatically during lay-offs.

People in my area are being laid off. Employees in my company are being laid off. My neighbor is out of a job right now. She was a supervisor in a major aerospace company for fourteen years before they recently shut down the Tulsa plant. The company is losing a lot of money, primarily due to the cutback in defense spending, and they had to consolidate what work they had left. The Tulsa operation became expendable. My neighbor now attends our local junior college in the hopes of learning new, and marketable, skills. In the meantime, the family must live on less.

It's a story that is, has been, and will be told by many people. People get jobs, and they lose jobs. It seems that business always chooses profits over people. The job with life-time security seems an ideal of the past; with a rapidly changing economy everyone in private business and in government work seems vulnerable. Budget cutting and profit-making take priority over people.

At least for workfaith believers, shouldn't the priority be people before profits?

Not necessarily. Both people and profits can be emphasized. They are not mutually exclusive. In fact, treating employees with genuine respect is one of the best strategies for making a profit. As we just saw with Jeff and Brenda, workfaith believers strive to love people and make a profit without one interfering with the other.

Reality, unfortunately, is not always so tidy. At times, tough choices have to be made, and the conflict between people and profits becomes very real. When a company loses money consistently, one of the choices that has to be made is whether laying off some workers is the only, or best, way to return to profitability.

In the final analysis, lay-offs are not contradictory to good workfaith principles.

The way a layoff takes place can make a big difference. One company's approach can be truly heartless—the message to all employees reflects the company's attitude that employees are only functionaries. Another company who is forced to make the same decision can do it with as much concern, regret, and assistance as they can offer. In both cases, the employees no longer have a job. But in the second example, respect for people remains constant even during this crisis. The final decision is based on the profit issue, but the concern for people is still evident—both to the laid-off employees and the remaining workers.

There are many other situations at work that pit profits against people. Promotions, job assignments, exceptions to standard policies, performance reviews, performance expectations—all ultimately are designed to help the company make a profit but all are also fertile ground for conflicts with people. Sometimes employees are undoubtedly treated unfairly. On the other hand, some employees who claim unfair treatment are selfish, immature, manipulative or power hungry themselves. The accusation that a company, bosses, or co-workers are so profit oriented that they ignore people is not proof that such behavior is true.

We may find ourselves in the middle of some of these complicated and emotional personnel conflicts. As true believers, we attempt to do the loving thing, even as we deliver necessary bad news, e.g. poor performance reviews, unpopular job assignments, less than expected pay raises, etc. The best, most loving way to handle these situations is not always clear, and even the most ardent workfaith believers can make mistakes in dealing with these highly charged conflicts.

The tension between people and profits will always be part of the work experience. The general workfaith principle attempts to maintain a balance between profit and people but, in the final analysis, the purpose of the workplace is not to employ people but to provide a product or service for a reasonable profit. That fundamental priority does not eliminate workfaith. It is simply one of the realities of this imperfect world, a world which God also chooses to inhabit.

Boring

Another dimension to this issue of people versus profit centers on the work experience itself. Some jobs are boring. I worked a few of them myself. There's no denying it. We can seek ways to change the boring nature of the job by attempting to become more involved in the decision making part of the workplace and by suggesting ways to improve the process. But, even if these efforts pay off, some jobs remain boring.

A workfaith approach to these jobs will not eliminate the boredom completely. But workfaith can add meaning to the work experience. By consciously connecting our boring, repetitious jobs to a larger context which includes the building of the kingdom and the mission of the Christian, we can make the work less boring.

Boredom usually takes place when we cannot see our current effort as part of anything significant. We see repetitious, isolated work as meaningless in itself and feel no pride or responsibility in whatever the final product or service will be. Employers have a duty to structure the work activities and to treat workers in such a way that this sense of isolation and meaninglessness is minimized. But even in the best of situations, some jobs are necessarily repetitious and potentially boring. By accepting the workfaith view of our jobs we can reduce the boredom.

This sense of boredom shows up in another way. How many times have you heard that "the only thing that is important to me about my job is my paycheck and my benefits. The rest of it is meaningless." That, once again, is boredom speaking.

Obviously, our paycheck and our benefits are a major part of our worklife. The paycheck determines our life style. We work so that we can pay our bills, and buy the things and services we need or want.

The issue of just pay is the first consideration. What is a just wage? How much pay for how much work? Answers and figures vary from job to job and country to country, so we can't pin down a figure. Workfaith calls for a just wage, whatever that figure is for a specific job.

But workfaith goes farther. Let's assume we receive a "just" wage. We may feel we deserve more, but we accept that our current wage is fair enough. The justice issue is basically settled.

Workfaith then raises this question: is it acceptable to work only for the pay?

No!

If pay is the only motivation, we are not able to integrate work with faith. Our actual daily labor is immaterial, if the paycheck is the only thing that really matters. Workfaith calls for a richer, more complete meaning to the work activity.

Don't get me wrong—the paycheck and the benefits are extremely important. It is certainly acceptable—from a workfaith point of view—to work for pay. Supporting oneself or a family, providing enough money for shelter, food, transportation, education and a reasonable style of life, are commendable workfaith goals. Sharing our income, through taxes and, voluntarily, through charitable contributions, with those people in need or to support common services are also valuable benefits of a paycheck. Getting paid is vital and a very legitimate motive for working.

But workfaith believers don't stop with this motivation. For us, the added dimension of the work activity, the forces at work and the people at work must all be included in any meaningful reflection on the value of work. Along with the pay, these other elements are essential in order to find and bring meaning to work. As a result, our work life is much richer, more rewarding and more relevant than people who work only for the money.

To help offset boredom and stress, most jobs offer some vacation time. Vacation provides a rest, an extended break from the responsibilities of work. Most of us need that break in order to explore different aspects of our personalities and to develop a more complete experience of life. The purpose of vacation is not limited to giving employes time off so they can come back and work better. Vacation respects the fact that employees are more than employees. We have other legitimate activities and relationships in life. We devote so much time and effort to our jobs that we deserve at least some time away from work in order to activate these other parts of life. Typically the longer we work in a job, the longer amounts of vacation we receive. All things considered, this approach to vacation appears to be just.

Scripture, too, supports the need for rest. Genesis 2:2-3 states it very clearly: "Since on the seventh day God was finished with the work he had been doing, he rested on the seventh day from all the work he had undertaken. So God blessed the seventh day and made it holy, because on it he rested from all the work he had done in creation."

The message here is that we need rest from our daily chores. But we also need some time to realign our priorities. God simply must come first even when we focus on our work duties. Time away from work is required to experience the many dimensions of God as well as the many dimensions of life.

Vacation is an extension of the daily and weekend break from work. Vacation is more extended and therefore offers a greater opportunity to truly get away from work-related responsibilities. For many of us it takes time to change from our work patterns in order to explore other facets of our personality and life. Vacation can more easily accomplish this change than evenings, weekends or other days off. Vacation, then, is critical to work and workfaith because it challenges us to recognize that work is not everything.

Workfaith, then, insists that our work need not be destructively boring. Our work is more than a way to get a paycheck. Workfaith also insists that we find God within our work experience. Vacation time helps us establish some balance between work and non-work life. The balance relieves the boredom that many workers complain about. Ultimately, each of us is responsible for eliminating this sense of boredom from our work. Workfaith can help in that process by discovering and bringing more meaning to work.

The Rich and the Unemployed

The profit motive has a very personal side. The dream of many people is to become wealthy. Whatever the motives are for this dream, the reality is that many people want to be rich. Some people will work hard to achieve this goal. Some will unscrupulously try anything for the sake of money, while others simply buy lottery tickets and hope to win big. How does this dream, this goal, fit into workfaith?

Riches are not evil in themselves, and the goal of becoming wealthy is not inherently wrong. The workfaith view of wealth is based on the teachings of Jesus. One passage that illustrates this outlook is the story of the rich man in Mark's gospel (10:17-25). The man asks Jesus what he must do to share in eternal life and Jesus tells him to keep the commandments. The man insists that he has kept the commandments all his life. Jesus does not dispute the man's claim, but then the Lord goes to the heart of the matter. "Jesus looked at him with love and told him, 'There is one thing more you must do. Go sell what you have and give to the poor; you will then have treasure in heaven. After that, come and follow me.' At these words the man's face fell. He went away sad, for he had many possessions" (Mk 10:21-22).

The primary issue with this man is not the fact of his wealth. The difficulty is that his identity is tied with his riches. He could not see himself without his money. He was a good man in terms of his moral life; he followed the commandments. But his values were such that he could not accept himself without his wealth. Being a follower of Jesus was not how he viewed himself. Being a rich man was his deepest identity. He could not change his basic identity enough to be a true follower of Jesus.

His fundamental problem is not greed. His fundamental problem is a misplaced personal identity.

That's the key to understanding the workfaith view of the dream to be wealthy. The trouble with riches is that they have a tendency to make us dependent on wealth, just like the man in the gospel. We begin to think of ourselves as "wealthy" and "rich". It becomes more difficult to think of ourselves as "servants", "dependent on God" and "humble." That's why Jesus proclaimed: "How hard it is for the rich to enter the kingdom of God!" (Mk 10:23).

On the other hand, if rich people are able to be aware of their dependence on God and grateful for their existence, accept their wealth as a gift, and in all matters maintain an identity that is founded on their faith in God, then their riches need not hinder them from being genuine disciples of Jesus. Riches are an added obstacle to faith but they do not automatically disqualify a person from the kingdom. In fact, the wealthy are in a position to support kingdom building projects and activities financially in a way other people simply can't do.

Workfaith, then, does not evaluate a job by how much money it provides, as the culture does. Society says that poor paying jobs are not as good as high paying jobs. Workfaith says that both the poor paying jobs and the high paying jobs contribute to the kingdom. How much they contribute depends to a large extent on the people who are working rather than the amount of money they generate. Once the basic justice issue is resolved, workfaith is not dependent on the amount of money earned. In fact, it is possible that a low paying job is more beneficial to the kingdom than a high paying job. Making lots of money, then, is an acceptable goal for workfaith believers, but only if the priorities are kept in place. For true believers, God must continue to come first, regardless of income.

On the other end of the profit scale are the poor and the unemployed. Workfaith applies to the unemployed also, but obviously it applies in a different way. In one sense, the job of the involuntarily unemployed is to find a job. I was never unemployed, but I was very close at one point in my life. I was working under a three year contract, and six months prior to the end of that contract, I told my boss that I was not going to renew my contract. I had "assurances" from a few "reliable sources" that I could have a choice of jobs. I gave so much notice because I wanted to help search, hire and train my replacement, which I did. But when the time came for me to leave, all my "assurances" came to a dead end. I was fortunate to sell cars for six months, at which time my former boss had a different position for me which I immediately accepted.

During the time between giving notice and starting my job as a car salesman, I was looking for a job. As millions of people know, finding the next job is a difficult task. It is often accompanied by feelings of hurt, bitterness, inadequacy and disappointment. I felt them all. A job hunt is essentially and necessarily a negative work activity. It is negative because the purpose of the search is only completed when a job is found. Until that time, everything is "No."

The key point from a workfaith perspective is that God is present to the unemployed as well as the employed. Unemployed workfaith believers will identify that presence and rely on it for comfort and encouragement during this very trying time. Usually people are unemployed through no fault of their own. The economy goes bad and the company has to lay off some employees. Seniority may determine who gets laid off. At times a particular function may be eliminated or consolidated with another function, and the corresponding workers are let go. Or the company is sold to another group who already have people performing that function. Maybe automation replaces workers. For government employees, budget cuts generally mean people cuts.

Regardless of how or why it happens, the result is that many people who are unemployed are in that situation even though they had nothing to do with it.

At these times, we can easily feel like victims. Workfaith believers in this position will identify with Jesus as victim and draw some consolation from the way he turned his suffering and death into resurrection. As bills mount up and benefits dwindle, as prospects continue to look bleak, as the possibility of working at greatly reduced wages becomes imminent, the discouragement can become overwhelming. At these times, it's hard to see any positive aspects of unemployment. But there are some, from a workfaith outlook. A life style change may be necessary, and it's possible that the values and life style prior to unemployment may have been too materialistic. Or perhaps there was little appreciation of the income that was previously earned.

Unemployment may offer us an opportunity to re-evaluate our values. Of course, in one sense, this condition is forced; we don't choose to be unemployed. On the other hand, what we do with our unemployment, how we react to it personally, what effect it has on our emotional and spiritual life, is ultimately a personal choice. While it would be unrealistic to thank God for the opportunity to be unemployed, it is possible to use this experience as a serious examination of some basic life style values. Valuable, critical questions can be asked—questions like: What do I really need to be happy? How much income must I have in order to survive? What really happens to me if I lose many of the things I have taken for granted? Can I view myself as a worthwhile, valuable person even when I am unemployed?

Answers to these and similar questions, asked at a time when experiencing unemployment, may prove extremely helpful for the rest of our lives. Without minimizing the hardships and sacrifices, both financial and emotional, associated with many cases of unemployment, it is still possible, from a workfaith point of view, to discover the presence of God in this circumstance and to benefit from the experience.

There is another aspect of being unemployed that touches on workfaith. Many times the unemployed are the recipients of government or charitable assistance. Unemployment checks, assistance in hunting for a new job, food stamps, charitable food gifts, clothes donations, etc. may be needed and accepted. But they may also be received with a sense of humiliation and wounded pride.

Workfaith believers approach this situation differently. We are grateful for the assistance, but we don't take advantage of it and we don't deny our need for it. We strive to be self-sufficient as soon as possible. But if service for others is an essential element of workfaith and Christianity, as it is, then some people will have to be recipients of that service. Being a grateful and genuine recipient of someone's service, whether it be personally and privately delivered or through a government program, is not easy for some people. The experience of unemployment may be a chance for us to learn gratitude without strings attached, humility without humiliation, and dignity without superficial trappings.

There are also people who choose unemployment: very wealthy people who don't have to work; people who are too lazy to work; people who truly can't find work; people who simply decide not to work and who choose to live a bare subsistence life; alcoholics and drug addicts who can't hold a job; people who are physically, mentally or emotionally unable to work; spouses or adult children who depend on someone else to work and earn enough to pay the bills; spouses whose work is dedicated to the family but who earn no income, etc.—all of these groups are unemployed according to the definition used here.

Circumstances vary from group to group, and from person to person. But for each group and person, there is a workfaith point of view. The loving presence of God is available to each of us in whatever we do. The process for discovering, identifying, nurturing and celebrating that presence is similar for these believers as it is for people who are employed in a paying job. Since God is everywhere, the Trinity is also available to these people.

Workaholics

From people who don't work at all, we move to workaholics. Some of these people are driven by the profit motive—they work very long hours in order to continually make more money. But there are others who like their work, find their greatest personal sense of accomplishment at work, and are bored and uninspired away from work. As with any other group, there are many motivations and variations among these workaholics. Some may do it because they enjoy it; others may work because of a sense of obligation, fear, or to avoid facing other responsibilities.

The motivation for working more than normal hours makes a difference on how workfaith believers respond to this situation. If the motivation is fear, an unbalanced sense of obligation or the belief that "I am indispensable," then the workaholic needs to examine this motivation and arrive at a more balanced view of life.

On the other hand, there are people who truly love their work. They have a job that challenges them, fully engages them, and offers personal rewards along with the financial compensation. They are perfectly willing to sacrifice some other personal activities in order to work more. They either don't have family responsibilities, or they have arrived at an acceptable arrangement with the family in terms of time spent together. They much prefer working to sitting at home and watching TV, having a hobby, or participating in a club or other civic, church or social activity. They don't need as much rest away from the job because the job is not a source of undue stress. They like what they do, and they don't need much time to take care of other responsibilities.

For these, people working and living go hand in hand.

From a workfaith perspective, there is nothing wrong with this chosen way of life. God must always be the basic priority in life, as is the case for every believer. But the fact that people choose to devote a large portion of their life to work does not automatically mean that God is pushed to the perimeter. In fact, genuine workfaith believers may have a closer relationship with God, through work, than other people who work a forty hour week. And their work doesn't have to be obviously religious, as in formal ministry, in order to experience God on the job. Workaholics who are also workfaith believers can find God at work just as easily as other people find God in other ways and settings.

There isn't just one way to experience life. Fortunately! Life's activities can be divided in many ways. Certain cautions are always in order: when there are family responsibilities, for example, these responsibilities must be accepted and met. God must always be first. Enough time must be used to balance life, at least to the extent that emotional, psychic and social damage is not done. Beyond these basic considerations, however, we can choose to spend a lot of time at work. More than likely, most of us will not make such a choice. But for those who do, it is possible to be a workaholic and a workfaith believer.

Kingdom Jobs

Some jobs are more obviously kingdom building than others. For example, some teachers in religiously oriented schools choose to teach in these schools because they can be more explicit about expressing their faith. The whole atmosphere of the school reflects a religious environment as well as an academic one. These teachers have the opportunity to build a community with conscious and deliberate appeals to religious values. It is probably easier for these workfaith believers to see the connection between their daily work and the building of the kingdom.

But this connection is not automatic, and the mere fact of being a teacher in a religious school does not guarantee this commitment or this level of faith. The institutional commitment to faith does not insure that each teacher is personally committed. And, in the final analysis, workfaith is personal. A teacher's true motives for teaching in a religious school may have little to do with personal faith. Therefore, even in those jobs that are more obviously kingdom building, individual workers may or may not take advantage of this aspect of their job.

It is best not to judge the level of an individual's workfaith by the job the person has. Real believers are needed in all jobs. All workers everywhere can expand the kingdom by following the principles of workfaith. In some positions, this expression of workfaith may be easier than in other positions. In some cases, the emphasis may be on the people at work while in other situations the focus may shift to the forces at work or the work activity itself. In any case, real believers are needed in all situations. The circumstances of the job may dictate various practical applications of workfaith, but the fact that some of these applications may be "easier" than others does not mean that the "harder" situations need less true believers. In fact, it can be argued that those jobs that seems less conducive to the kingdom are precisely the jobs that demand "real" believers, people who can identify the kingdom building value of the work, improve the negative forces at work and relate to people in a way that reflects gospel values.

The choice of jobs is a personal one. Many people take a job because that's what is available at the time they need a job. That is certainly understandable. I did that myself a few times in my life.

Once on the job, however, workfaith believers attempt to make the most of it, not only in terms of our personal adjustment but also in terms of our faith. In other words, if the job is truly a matter of choice, we will "choose" it personally after we are in it. Or we could seek a different position. The point is that we adjust to the job and continually seek to discover the presence of God at work. If we have a choice of jobs, we make that choice based on a number of factors, not the least of which is our judgment of how well we will be able to integrate our faith with our work. But we know that all jobs have the potential for workfaith.

Stockholders and Taxpayers

There are three distinct groups who have a direct interest in a company's product or service. First of all, there are the consumers, the people who pay for the product or benefit from the service. Secondly, there are the employees who supply the product or service. And thirdly, there are the stockholders who provide the funds necessary to start and operate a business. All three groups have an interest in the profit motive.

Here we turn our attention to the stockholders. In government agencies, taxpayers provide the funding. While stockholders and taxpayers are very different in how they finance an operation, they are alike in that they do support work activity with financial resources.

Workfaith believers who are stockholders and/or taxpayers have responsibilities with regard to the product or service our money helps support.

As taxpayers we will insist that our money be spent wisely. Politics, and politicians, enter the picture because it's in the political arena that decisions are made regarding taxes. Balancing the needs of the country with available funding is one of the major responsibilities of all politicians. Workfaith politicians will incorporate their beliefs in a loving God, and a corresponding code of ethics, into their political decisions. By definition politicians are often required to compromise their positions in order to achieve a consensus. Workfaith politicians will not compromise to such an extent that they sacrifice basic faith and moral commitments.

Workfaith taxpayers will take an active role in the political process because one of the principles of workfaith challenges us to use our money as good stewards. We want to know how our money is spent and protest loudly if this money is spent on projects that are inconsistent with the gospel or if money is wasted. The basis of the protest is not only that we don't like the way our money is used; there's more to this than a disagreement about program funding. The key issue revolves around the use of money in order to promote the kingdom of God. The goals of the kingdom need not be inconsistent with the goals of the government. In fact, the essential goals of government—safety, aid for the needy, policy and law that protects the rights of all citizens, infrastructure needs, common concerns, etc.—parallel many of the goals of the kingdom. The kingdom, of course, includes other goals related to the spiritual life. But there are many areas where the goals of the government and the goals of the kingdom coincide.

We are aware of these converging goals and support those government projects that reflect these kingdom goals. While the method to reach these goals can be debated by honest people, it is still significant that these goals are not only political aspirations but many of them also nurture the needs of the kingdom.

In business, workfaith stockholders are interested in the whole operation of the company, at least in general terms. In other words, these stockholders do not limit their interest to the financial rewards they expect to gain. Workfaith stockholders focus also on the nature of the product or service the company offers and how well it delivers on its product/service. They look for more than money and what they can get out of the company. As much as possible, they are not remote. Their role is not to "run" the daily operation but they are familiar enough to know that nothing is flagrantly immoral or contradictory to the principles of the kingdom.

Many stockholders have mutual funds, i.e. they invest in many companies, and it is impossible to be active in all of these operations. These workfaith stockholders invest their money through a broker or advisor they trust. These stockholders inform their broker of their concerns and insist that their money be invested only in those companies that reflect principles consistent with the gospel.

Stockholders/taxpayers have a critical role in the experience of work. Their financial support is absolutely essential to the workplace. As such, they need to avoid the temptation to look only at the money side of the operation and to remain remote from the product or service the company provides. As with every other phase of the work experience, workfaith stockholders seek to discover and celebrate the presence of God in their investments.

Pass It On

Where do we go from here? How can the message of workfaith be spread to other people?

A number of things need to be done. These initial comments about workfaith need to be discussed and examined by other believers, theologians, spiritual directors and especially by people who work in the secular world. These further reflections and shared experiences will bring clarifications, implications, and applications of the basic message presented here. As long as this dialogue stays focused on the practical work experience of millions of people and their genuine desire to integrate faith with work, progress will be made. To be genuinely helpful, the discussion must remain practical, responding to and clarifying the real issues of real workers.

Continuing prayer is essential. Through prayer, we will discover the presence of God at work and the many implications of that presence. Prayer provides the opportunity for expressing gratitude to God for work activities, the work itself, the forces at work and the people at work. Prayer makes it possible to see God more clearly and to see ourselves more clearly. In and through prayer we become more aware of God. This awareness is vital in order to discover the presence of God, through workfaith, at work.

There are many ways that the theme of workfaith can be spread. Churches can sponsor small group sessions where searching believers discuss and identify the presence of God in their workplace. Sessions for people who have the same or similar kinds of jobs could meet and clarify the way their work activity connects with the kingdom and what the specific forces are that shape their work experience. They can seek ways to refine this work activity and reshape these forces so the workplace can more clearly represent the kingdom of God and the Trinitarian community. These groups can then record and share their insights with similar groups in other churches.

Other books can be written, some perhaps more theoretical while others focus on the practical "how-tos" of workfaith, including testimonies of people who experience workfaith. Sessions for the clergy can be conducted. Workfaith themes can enter into homilies more frequently. Permanent deacons can be recruited to reflect upon and develop workfaith topics. This message can become part of seminary and permanent deacon training. Workers can discuss these issues at lunch, or other appropriate times. Seminars and workshops can be held.

In order to help facilitate and coordinate the initial response to workfaith, I will be happy to receive any mail related to the topic of this book. "The Workfaith Institute," which I am establishing, is committed to promoting the goals of workfaith. Short or long articles, comments, questions, disagreements, clarifications, further aspects of the theme, concerns, or any other suggestions are all welcome. I will gather them, organize them, respond to them and distribute them in whatever way is appropriate. Perhaps a newsletter will be necessary. The key is to create a dialogue and then communicate the evolving results of this dialogue to an ever widening circle of people.

You can send any correspondence to: The Workfaith Institute, 1304 E. Dover Street, Broken Arrow, Oklahoma 74012.

It is important to pursue this question of how God is present at work, and what we can do with it and about it. Most of us spend a large amount of time and energy in the workplace. Most of us have difficulty integrating this work experience with our faith. Workfaith centers on this problem and offers a way to deal with this complicated, but critical, aspect of life.

God does not want to be ignored at work. We have the opportunity and the responsibility to respond to God on the job. Workfaith offers that opportunity.

Study Questions

1. *In your opinion, how are competition and community related? Can they co-exist successfully? If so, what does it take to balance competition and community.*

2. *How significant is "getting a paycheck" to you? How significant are other factors (job satisfaction, work hours, co-workers, etc.) to you? If you were financially secure, what kind of work would you do?*

3. *If you have ever been unemployed, share that experience. What are the workfaith aspects of unemployment?*

4. *How has reading this book and/or discussing it with your group deepened your relationship with God?*

5. *Summarize the benefits you have experienced from your focus on workfaith. What more would you like to do on this topic (e.g., make a retreat, attend a workshop, do more reading, pray more about these themes, continue a discussion, write your own reflection, etc.)?*